Ethical Hacking Techniques and Countermeasures for Cybercrime Prevention

Nabie Y. Conteh
Southern University at New Orleans, USA

A volume in the Advances in
Information Security, Privacy, and
Ethics (AISPE) Book Series

Published in the United States of America by
>   IGI Global
>   Information Science Reference (an imprint of IGI Global)
>   701 E. Chocolate Avenue
>   Hershey PA, USA 17033
>   Tel: 717-533-8845
>   Fax: 717-533-8661
>   E-mail: cust@igi-global.com
>   Web site: http://www.igi-global.com

Library of Congress Cataloging-in-Publication Data

Names: Conteh, Nabie, 1960- editor.
Title: Ethical hacking techniques and countermeasures for cybercrime
   prevention / Nabie Conteh, editor.
Description: Hershey, PA : Information Science Reference, an imprint of IGI
   Global, 2021. | Includes bibliographical references and index. |
   Summary: "This edited book serves as a guide for certification training,
   the study of countermeasures to prevent and stop cybercrimes,
   cyberterrorism, cybertheft, identity theft and computer related
   crimes"-- Provided by publisher.
Identifiers: LCCN 2020044218 (print) | LCCN 2020044219 (ebook) | ISBN
   9781799865049 (hardcover) | ISBN 9781799865056 (paperback) | ISBN
   9781799865063 (ebook)
Subjects: LCSH: Penetration testing (Computer security) | Computer
   crimes--Prevention.
Classification: LCC QA76.9.A25 E867 2021 (print) | LCC QA76.9.A25 (ebook)
   | DDC 005.8--dc23
LC record available at https://lccn.loc.gov/2020044218
LC ebook record available at https://lccn.loc.gov/2020044219

This book is published in the IGI Global book series Advances in Information Security, Privacy, and Ethics (AISPE) (ISSN: 1948-9730; eISSN: 1948-9749)

British Cataloguing in Publication Data
A Cataloguing in Publication record for this book is available from the British Library.

All work contributed to this book is new, previously-unpublished material.
The views expressed in this book are those of the authors, but not necessarily of the publisher.

For electronic access to this publication, please contact: eresources@igi-global.com.

Advances in Information Security, Privacy, and Ethics (AISPE) Book Series

ISSN:1948-9730
EISSN:1948-9749

Editor-in-Chief: Manish Gupta, State University of New York, USA

MISSION

As digital technologies become more pervasive in everyday life and the Internet is utilized in ever increasing ways by both private and public entities, concern over digital threats becomes more prevalent.

The **Advances in Information Security, Privacy, & Ethics (AISPE) Book Series** provides cutting-edge research on the protection and misuse of information and technology across various industries and settings. Comprised of scholarly research on topics such as identity management, cryptography, system security, authentication, and data protection, this book series is ideal for reference by IT professionals, academicians, and upper-level students.

COVERAGE

- Cyberethics
- Technoethics
- Computer ethics
- Privacy Issues of Social Networking
- Information Security Standards
- Risk Management
- Device Fingerprinting
- Privacy-Enhancing Technologies
- Security Information Management
- IT Risk

IGI Global is currently accepting manuscripts for publication within this series. To submit a proposal for a volume in this series, please contact our Acquisition Editors at Acquisitions@igi-global.com or visit: http://www.igi-global.com/publish/.

Titles in this Series

For a list of additional titles in this series, please visit:
http://www.igi-global.com/book-series/advances-information-security-privacy-ethics/37157

Enabling Blockchain Technology for Secure Networking and Communications
Adel Ben Mnaouer (Canadian University Dubai, UAE) and Lamia Chaari Fourati (University of Sfax, Tunisia)
Information Science Reference • © 2021 • 339pp • H/C (ISBN: 9781799858393) • US $215.00

Multidisciplinary Approach to Modern Digital Steganography
Sabyasachi Pramanik (Haldia Institute of Technology, India) Mangesh Manikrao Ghonge (Sandip Foundation's Institute of Technology and Research Centre, India) Renjith V. Ravi (MEA Engineering College, India) and Korhan Cengiz (Trakya University, Turkey)
Information Science Reference • © 2021 • 380pp • H/C (ISBN: 9781799871606) • US $195.00

Strategic Approaches to Digital Platform Security Assurance
Yuri Bobbert (ON2IT BV, The Netherlands & Antwerp Management School, University of Antwerp, Belgium) Maria Chtepen (BNP Paribas Group, Belgium) Tapan Kumar (Cognizant, The Netherlands) Yves Vanderbeken (DXC, Belgium) and Dennis Verslegers (Orange Cyberdefense, Belgium)
Information Science Reference • © 2021 • 394pp • H/C (ISBN: 9781799873679) • US $195.00

Security and Privacy Solutions for the Internet of Energy
Mohamed Amine Ferrag (Guelma University, Algeria)
Information Science Reference • © 2021 • 325pp • H/C (ISBN: 9781799846161) • US $195.00

Privacy and Security Challenges in Location Aware Computing
P. Shanthi Saravanan (J.J. College of Engineering and Technology, Tiruchirappalli, India) and S. R. Balasundaram (National Institute of Technology, Tiruchirappalli, India)
Information Science Reference • © 2021 • 298pp • H/C (ISBN: 9781799877561) • US $195.00

For an entire list of titles in this series, please visit:
http://www.igi-global.com/book-series/advances-information-security-privacy-ethics/37157

701 East Chocolate Avenue, Hershey, PA 17033, USA
Tel: 717-533-8845 x100 • Fax: 717-533-8661
E-Mail: cust@igi-global.com • www.igi-global.com

Table of Contents

Detailed Table of Contents

This chapter will discuss the important topic of ethical hacking, also known as penetration testing. It will start by explaining the constituents of ethical hacking: scope and goal setting, exploitation, and documentation. The authors will define and explain the reasons for the rapid rise in cyber-crimes and their socio-economic impact. It will further discuss the steps involved in ethical hacking, who is allowed to conduct ethical hacking, its importance, and the role it plays in deterring future and potential hackers. The chapter will analyze the various types of malware and the steps to follow to become an ethical hacker. It will further describe social engineering, the types of cyber-attacks, the phases of attack, testing for vulnerabilities, and it will put forward a list of countermeasures. The chapter will end by detailing the steps to be taken in the documentation process and crafting the executive summary.

The broad objective of this study is to evaluate the vulnerabilities of an organization's information technology infrastructure, which include hardware and software systems, transmission media, local area networks, wide area networks, enterprise networks, intranets, and its use of the internet to cyber intrusions. To achieve this objective, the chapter explains the importance of social engineering in network intrusions and cyber-theft and the reasons for the rapid expansion of cybercrime. The chapter also includes a complete description and definition of social engineering, the role it plays in network intrusion and cyber identity theft, a discussion of the reasons for the rise in cybercrimes, and their impact on organizations. In closing the authors recommend some preventive measures and possible solutions to the threats and vulnerabilities of social engineering. The chapter concludes that while technology has a role to play in reducing the impact of social engineering attacks, the vulnerability resides with human behavior, human impulses, and psychological predispositions.

This chapter is primarily intended to firstly define and review the literature in cybersecurity and vividly shed light on the mechanisms involved in the social engineering phenomenon. It will discuss the various attempts at network intrusion and the steps typically taken in the implementation of cyber-thefts. The chapter will provide the rationale behind the justification of why humans are considered to be the weakest link in these attacks. The study will also explain the reasons for the rise in cybercrimes and their impact on organizations. In closing, the chapter will put forward some recommendations to serve as preventative measures and solutions to the threats and vulnerabilities posed by cyber-attacks. Finally, measures, such as conducting regular, thorough, and relevant awareness training, frequent drills, and realistic tests, will be addressed with a view to maintaining a steady focus on the overall discipline of the organization, thereby hardening the component of the network that is the softest by nature—the human vulnerability factor.

This chapter takes an in-depth look into the research literature to analyze and evaluate the role that social engineering plays in network intrusion and cybertheft. It will also discuss preventive measures and solutions to the threats and vulnerabilities that present themselves in the process of social engineering attacks. Social engineering is a means of stealing private data through tactics that make the victim feel comfortable to give their data. This kind of attack can cost individuals and organizations millions of dollars and block their access to data. The articles present multiple statistics that prove that the risk of social engineering attacks on individuals or organizations has increased tremendously. This new wave of communication has given hackers many opportunities to threaten security by tracking your email, phone, social networks, etc. Information detailing how users can be more aware of ways to protect their private information from attackers will also be presented.

Chapter 5

In the modern age of technological innovation, organizations are evolving rapidly due to the abundance of opportunities. This evolution has provided organizations with the ability to leverage technology for their benefit; however, cybersecurity risks have also developed due to the emerging trends. As the software industry faces a surge of emerging trends, it is critical to address the impeding threats to our cybersecurity infrastructure. The computer software industry is classified under the North American Industry Classification System (NAICS) code 511210 for software publishers. The software development market has experienced an exponential growth as a shift to the cloud has rendered a greater need for cutting edge technology, and this trend is projected to continue.

Chapter 6

Cybersecurity is an ever-evolving area of technology. As such, there will always be myriad trends to consider. Through the progression of cybersecurity comes the increased need for organizations to keep pace with the rapid development of technology. However, the current skills gap of cybersecurity professionals has overwhelmingly become a cause for concern. The spread of cloud computing has created a need for new cloud forensics procedures, and the use of internet-connected medical devices has added concerns for the information security structure of many organizations. In order to resolve these issues, proper vulnerability testing and implementation of new processes to keep up with the changes in technology have to be introduced to reduce the possibility of hacking incidents and aid in remediation. If more organizations leverage the skills and personnel available to them, there are ways to reduce the skills gap and other issues affecting cybersecurity.

Chapter 7

Previous literature has investigated if mobile applications unregulated by the United States, such as Tik-Tok, can have a detrimental impact regarding the vulnerability of personal identifiable information of their daily users and are therefore worthy of banned designation for consumer use in the United States. The research conducted in these findings aimed to assess the benefits and downsides of user-permitted data collection from mobile applications such as Tik-Tok including whether Tik-Tok indeed poses a serious national security threat due to its potential exploitation from foreign governments, therefore warranting government escalation from being closely monitored to banned status. This chapter's research also consisted of analyzing emerging trends in the mitigation of data security of consumer devices industry in the instances of cloud computing, 5G implementation in home automation, and mobile applications privacy. Previous findings implicate the potential vulnerability of PII in mobile applications and support the notion of Tik-Tok becoming banned by the United States.

Chapter 8
*Sahar A. El-Rahman, Computer Science Department, Princess Nourah
Bint Abdulrahman University, Riyadh, Saudi Arabia & Electrical
Engineering Department, Benha University, Cairo, Egypt*

Due to internet development, data transfer becomes faster and easier to transmit and receive different data types. The possibility of data loss or data modification by a third party is high. So, designing a model that allows stakeholders to share their data confidently over the internet is urgent. Steganography is a term used to hide information and an attempt to conceal the existence of embedded information in different types of multimedia. In this chapter, a steganography model is proposed to embed an image into a cover image based on DWT approach as the first phase. Then, the embedded secret image is extracted from the stego-image as the second phase. Model performance was evaluated based on signal noise ratio (SNR), PSNR, and MSE (mean square error). The proposed steganographic model based on DWT is implemented to hide confidential images about a nuclear reactor and military devices. The findings indicate that the proposed model provides a relatively high embedding payload with no visual distortion in the stego-image. It improves the security and maintains the hidden image correctness.

Chapter 9
*Nabie Y. Conteh, Southern University at New Orleans, USA
Quinnesha N. Staton, University of Maryland Global Campus, USA*

The purpose of this chapter is to explore and address the socio-economic impact of identity thefts and cybercrime in general. The chapter will further explain the various ways employed in their implementation. The chapter will also put forward ways to prevent the threats and vulnerabilities of the attacks. The study will also recommend solutions to stop and/or mitigate the consequences of cyber-thefts. The study will define social engineering as well as provide various social engineering tactic. The chapter will also discuss the reasons for the rise in cybercrime. Such reasons will include financial gain, revenge, as well as non-financial gains. Also cited are examples that demonstrate the capabilities of cybercriminal. The chapter will also provide justification for the reasons behind the cumbersome task and failure in instituting a lasting solution to the criminal activities. Finally, this chapter will close with a conclusion on the economic implications of social engineering on the general cyberwar on cybercrime at the national and global levels.

Chapter 10

C. V. Anchugam, BCA Department, Vidyavahini First Grade College, Bengaluru, India

Cyber security provides protection against theft of data, protects computers from theft, minimizes computer freezing, provides privacy for users, and offers strict regulation. Firewalls can be difficult to configure correctly. Faultily configured firewalls may prohibit users from performing any behavior on the internet before the firewall is properly installed, and you will continue to upgrade the latest software to retain current protection. Cyber protection can be expensive for ordinary users. This is chapter helps to understand phases of attacks and types of attacks. Ethical hacking simulates a malicious attack without trying to cause damage. If you need to understand the countermeasures, first you need to understand the phases of an attack. It is necessary to comprehend the steps to counter an attack once it is detected and stop the attack before it reaches the next phase. In general, there are five phases that make up an attack such as reconnaissance, scanning, gaining access, maintaining access, covering tracks.

Chapter 11

Nabie Y. Conteh, Southern University at New Orleans, USA
DeAngela "Dee" Sword, University of Maryland Global Campus, USA

Social engineering attacks have emerged to become one of the most problematic tactics used against businesses today. Social engineers employ both human-based and computer-based tactics to successfully compromise their targeted networks. This chapter will discuss the basics of social engineering and what it means today. It will explain some common attack methods like baiting, phishing, pretexting, quid pro quo, tailgating, and dumpster diving. It will then highlight the impact social engineering has had on the rise in cybercrime and why threat actors have grown more innovative. Finally, this chapter will discuss what multi-layer defense or defense in depth is and offer countermeasures that can be enforced to defend against social engineering attacks.

Preface

Welcome to *Ethical Hacking Techniques and Countermeasures for Cybercrime Prevention.*

Cybersecurity is the practice of protecting systems, computing devices and data assets that are connected to the Internet, the interconnected network of networks. These include but not limited to hardware, software, data centers, databases and data assets. It is geared towards protecting them not only from cyber-threats but eliminating any all vulnerabilities. They include the methods and techniques that are utilized by individuals and enterprises alike with a view to protecting the computers, servers, networks, web applications, mobile devices and the data stored on these devices from black hat attackers (with malicious intent) and to stop against unauthorized access.

The book starts with an introductory chapter that will cover the concept of computer security, data assets, and threats. The concepts of the CIA (Confidentiality, Integrity and Availability) triad will be addressed as well as risks and vulnerabilities. The book will also cover several cybersecurity related areas such as authentication, access control and related topics which would possibly include Cryptography, the art of secret writing, which serves as a tool for protecting against security threats. It is an attempt at disguising data to prevent reading, modification and fabrication of data.

CHAPTER BREAKDOWN

Chapter 1, "Ethical Hacking, Threats, Vulnerabilities, and Their Countermeasures in Cybersecurity," introduces the important topic of ethical hacking, also known as penetration testing It will start by explaining the constituents of ethical hacking: scope and goal setting, exploitation and documentation. It also defines and explains the reasons for the rapid rise in cyber-crimes and their socio-economic impact. It will further discuss the steps involved in ethical hacking, it will also discuss who is allowed to conduct ethical hacking, its importance and the role it plays in deterring future and potential hackers. The chapter will analyze the various types of malware and the steps to follow to become an ethical hacker. It will further describe social engineering, the types of cyber-attacks, the phases of attack, testing for vulnerabilities and put forward a list of countermeasures. In closing, the chapter will end by detailing the steps to be taken in the documentation process and crafting the executive summary.

Chapter 2, "Cybersecurity Risks, Vulnerabilities, and Countermeasures to Prevent Social Engineering Attacks," evaluates the vulnerabilities of an organization's information technology infrastructure, which include hardware and software systems, transmission media, local area networks, wide area networks, enterprise networks, Intranets, and its use of the Internet to cyber intrusions. To achieve this objective, the chapter explains the importance of social engineering in network intrusions and cyber-theft and the reasons for the rapid expansion of cybercrime. The chapter also includes a complete description and definition of social engineering, the role it plays in network intrusion and cyber identity theft, a discussion of the reasons for the rise in cybercrime and their impact on organizations. In closing the authors recommend some preventive measures and possible solutions to the threats and vulnerabilities of social engineering. The chapter concludes that while technology has a role to play in reducing the impact of social engineering attacks, the vulnerability resides with human behavior, human impulses and psychological predispositions.

Chapter 3, "The Unprecedented Rise in Cybercrime and the Role of the Human Vulnerability Factor," is primarily intended to firstly define and review the literature in cybersecurity and vividly shed light on the mechanisms involved in the social engineering phenomenon. It will discuss the various attempts at network intrusion and the steps typically taken in the implementation of cyber-thefts. The chapter will provide the rationale behind the justification of why humans are considered to be the weakest link in these attacks. The study will also explain the reasons for the rise in cybercrimes and their impact on Organizations. In closing, the chapter will put forward some recommendations to serve as preventative measures and solutions to the threats and vulnerabilities posed by cyber-attacks. Finally, measures, such as conducting regular, thorough, and relevant awareness training, frequent drlls and realistic tests will be addressed with a view to maintaining a steady focus on the overall discipline of the organization thereby hardening that component of the network that is the softest by nature—the human vulnerability factor.

Chapter 4, "Evaluating the Impact of Cybertheft through Social Engineering and Network Intrusions," takes an in-depth into the research literature to analyze and evaluate the role that social engineering plays in network intrusion and cybertheft. It will also discuss preventive measures and solutions to the threats and vulnerabilities that present themselves in the process of social engineering attacks. Social engineering is a means of stealing private data through tactics that make the victim feel comfortable to give their data. This kind of attack can cause individuals and organizations millions of dollars to regain access to their data. The articles present multiple statistics that prove that in recent years, the risk of social engineering happening to an individual or organization has increased tremendously. Research has discovered that the recent rise of attacks correlates to data being transmitted digitally. This new wave of communication has given hackers many opportunities to threaten security by tracking your email, phone, social networks, etc. Information detailing how users can be more aware of ways to protect their private information from attackers will also be presented.

Chapter 5 is "Industry Trends in Computer Software." In the modern age of technological innovation, organizations are evolving rapidly due to the abundance of opportunities. This evolution has provided organizations with the ability to leverage technology for their benefit, however, cybersecurity risks have also developed due to the emerging trends. As the software industry faces a surge of emerging trends, it is critical to address the impeding threats to our cybersecurity infrastructure. The computer software industry is classified under the North American Industry Classification System (NAICS) code 511210 for Software Publishers. The software development market has experienced an exponential growth as a shift to the cloud has rendered a greater need for cutting edge technology and this trend is projected to continue.

Chapter 6 is "The Analysis of Top Cyber Investigation Trends." Cybersecurity is an ever-evolving area of technology. As such, there will always be a myriad of trends to consider. Through the progression of cybersecurity comes the increased need for organizations to keep pace with the rapid development of technology. However, the current skills gap of cybersecurity professionals has overwhelmingly become a cause for concern. The spread of cloud computing has created a need for new cloud forensics procedures, and the use of internet-connected medical devices has added concerns for the information security structure of many organizations. In order to resolve these issues, proper vulnerability testing and implementation of new processes to keep up with the changes in technology have to be introduced to reduce the possibility of hacking incidents and aid in remediation. If more organizations leverage the skills and personnel available to them, there are ways to reduce the skills gap and other issues affecting cybersecurity.

Chapter 7 is "Emerging Trends in the Mitigation of Data Security of Consumer Devices Industry." Previous literature has investigated if mobile applications unregulated by the United States, such as Tik-Tok, can have a detrimental impact regarding the vulnerability of personal identifiable information of its daily users and is therefore worthy of banned designation for consumer use in the United States. The research conducted in these findings are aimed to assess the benefits and downsides of user-permitted data collection from mobile applications such as Tik-Tok. Including whether Tik-Tok indeed poses a serious national security threat due to its potential exploitation from foreign governments, therefore warranting government escalation from being closely monitored to banned status. This chapter's research also consisted of analyzing emerging trends in the Mitigation of Data Security of Consumer Devices industry in the instances of Cloud computing, 5G implementation in home automation, and mobile applications privacy. Previous findings implicate the potential vulnerability of PII in mobile applications supports the notion of Tik-Tok becoming banned by the United States.

Chapter 8 is "DWT-Based Steganography for Images Transmission." Due to internet development, data transfer becomes faster and easier to transmit and receive different data types. The possibility of data loss or data modification by a third party is high. So, designing a model that allows stakeholders to share their data confidently over the internet is urgent. Steganography is a term used to hiding information and an attempt to conceal the existence of embedded information in different types of multimedia. In this chapter, a steganography model proposed to embed an image into a cover image based on DWT approach as the 1st phase. Then, the embedded secret image is extracted from the stego-image as 2nd phase. Model performance was evaluated based on Signal Noise Ratio (SNR), PSNR, and MSE (Mean Square Error). The proposed steganographic model based on DWT is implemented to hide confidential images about a nuclear reactor and military devices. The findings indicate that the proposed model provides a relatively high embedding payload with no visual distortion in the stego-image, whereas, improve the security and maintains the hidden image correctness, Image Steganography, Spatial Domain Techniques, Transform Domain Techniques Keywords: Discrete Wavelet Transform, Media Transmission, Information Security, Data hiding, Cryptography.

Chapter 9 is "The Socio-Economic Impact of Identity Thefts and Cybercrime: Preventive Measures and Solutions." The purpose of this chapter is to explore and address the socio-economic impact of identity thefts and cybercrime in general. The chapter will further explain the various ways employed in their implementation. The chapter will also put forward ways to prevent the threats and vulnerabilities of the attacks. The study will also recommend solutions to stop and or mitigate the consequences of cyber-thefts. The study will define social engineering as well as provide various social engineering tactic. The chapter will also discuss the reasons for the rise in cybercrime. Such reasons will include financial gain, revenge, as well as non-financial gains. Also cited are examples that demonstrate the capabilities of cybercriminal. The chapter will also provide justification for the reasons behind the cumbersome task and failure in instituting a lasting solution to the criminal activities. Finally, this chapter will close with a conclusion on the economic implications of social engineering on the general cyberwar on cybercrime at the national and global levels.

In general, while losses due to cybercrime are troubling, they do not directly pose as a threat to national security, except to the extent that international cybercrime allows potential opponents to train and maintain proxy forces at the expense of others.

Chapter 10 is "Essential of Security Elements and Phases of Hacking Attacks." Cyber Security provides protection against theft of data, protects computers from theft, minimizing computer freezing, provides privacy for users, it offers strict regulation, and it's difficult to work with non-technical people. Firewalls can be difficult to configure correctly, faulty configured firewalls may prohibit users from performing any behavior on the Internet before the Firewall is properly installed, and you will continue to upgrade the latest software to retain protection current, Cyber Protection can be expensive for ordinary users. This is chapter is help to understand phases of attacks and types of attacks. Ethical hacking simulates a malicious attack without trying to cause damage. If you need to understand the countermeasures, first you need to understand the phases of an attack. It is necessary to comprehend the steps of countering an attack once it is detected, and stop the attack before it reaches the next phase. In general, there are 5 phases that make up an attack such as reconnaissance, scanning, gaining access, maintaining access, covering tracks.

Chapter 11 is "The Dynamics of Social Engineering and Cybercrime in the Digital Age." Social engineering attacks have emerged to become one of the most problematic tactics used against businesses today. Social engineers employ both human based and computer based tactics to successfully compromise their targeted networks. This chapter will discuss the basics of social engineering and what it means today. It will explain some common attack methods like baiting, phishing, pretexting, quid pro quo, tailgating and dumpster diving. It will then highlight the impact social engineering has had on the rise in cybercrime and why threat actors have grown more innovative. Finally, this chapter will discuss what Multi-Layer Defense or Defense in Depth is and offer countermeasures that can be enforced to defend against social engineering attacks.

Acknowledgment

I would like to first and foremost extend my thanks to the team of Editors at IGI Global for the opportunity to publish with them, as well as the Book Development Coordinator, Ms. Maria Rohde for her patience and understanding in the submission and handling of the manuscript.

Let me also express my gratitude and appreciation to my former co-Advisors, Dr. Carolyn Seaman and Dr. Guisseppi Forgionne at the University of Maryland, Baltimore County (UMBC) for setting me on the path to this scholarly journey of teaching and research in academia.

I am appreciative of and grateful to the Executive Vice President-Chancellor, Dr. James H. Ammons at the Southern University at New Orleans for his leadership as well as the emphasis he is devoting to the area of cybersecurity. The list is too long to mention but I would like to recognize my colleagues and former students at Southern University at New Orleans in particular and at the entire Southern University System.

This book is dedicated to the memory of my late dad, Alhaji Abdul Rahman Conteh, who taught me to work hard and to strive to excel and my mother, Haja Ramatu Conteh in recognition of the immeasurable and crucial role they both played in my entire life and education. Without them, I would have never made it to this point. I am therefore grateful to them for their unconditional love.

Finally, I would like to extend my many grateful thanks to my wife, Jamila, my two children, Abdul and Rahma; as well as Soukaina and Zakaria for their love, patience and understanding; my siblings, Mariama Seray Charm, Amadu Wurie, Soribah Wurie, Aisha and Fatima for their love and support.

Nabie Y. Conteh
Southern University at New Orleans, USA

Chapter 1
Ethical Hacking, Threats, and Vulnerabilities in Cybersecurity

Nabie Y. Conteh
Southern University at New Orleans, USA

ABSTRACT

This chapter will discuss the important topic of ethical hacking, also known as penetration testing. It will start by explaining the constituents of ethical hacking: scope and goal setting, exploitation, and documentation. The authors will define and explain the reasons for the rapid rise in cyber-crimes and their socio-economic impact. It will further discuss the steps involved in ethical hacking, who is allowed to conduct ethical hacking, its importance, and the role it plays in deterring future and potential hackers. The chapter will analyze the various types of malware and the steps to follow to become an ethical hacker. It will further describe social engineering, the types of cyber-attacks, the phases of attack, testing for vulnerabilities, and it will put forward a list of countermeasures. The chapter will end by detailing the steps to be taken in the documentation process and crafting the executive summary.

INTRODUCTION

What Is Ethical Hacking?

Ethical hacking is sometimes known as penetration testing or pen testing. It is a legal way of breaking into computers and devices to test the strength of the defenses of organizations. In order to protect yourself from an attack, you need to know and understand how enemy works and fights against you. It is both and challenging and

DOI: 10.4018/978-1-7998-6504-9.ch001

exciting to pursue a career in ethical hacking as you are seen as playing the role of the good guy who is paid to protect the client (Webopedia, 2021).

It is an extremely important as most companies nowadays are networked and constantly sharing and exchanging data and information. The most valuable assets that companies possess are the intellectual assets and therefore they need to be protected from external threats as well as become hardened to eliminate all potential vulnerabilities which may cause the company networks to be attacked.

Companies engage ethical hackers to identify vulnerabilities in their systems. From the penetration tester's point of view, there is no downside: If you hack in past the current defenses, you've given the client a chance to close the hole before an attacker discovers it. If you don't find anything, your client is even happier because they now get to declare their systems "secure enough that even paid hackers couldn't break into it." Win-win!

There has to be consent from the party being hacked. Without permission to hack, the attempt at hacking or breaking into a computer system, hacking is considered an illegal offense that can result in prison time and heavy fines (Grimes, 2019)

Figure 1.
Image credits: LinkedIn

According to ethical hacker Roger A. Grimes in CSO, ethical hacking consists of three steps:

1. Scope and goal setting
2. Exploitation
3. Documentation

The scope and goal setting step involves the actual terms of the contract. These entail the what, the when, the where, and the how an ethical hacker would attempt to breach the system of an organization. To define this step in detail, it involves defining the target and timeframe of the penetration testing.

Exploitation is the step wherein the ethical hacker attempts to break into the target computer system. Hackers are sometimes required to take screenshots of this process or even film themselves as they attempt to hack. These resources can be of use to organizations and the ethical hackers alike as they work towards the final step, documentation.

Documentation is the step wherein the ethical hacker is required to prepares a detailed report for the organization. The contents of this report varies, but in general, ethical hackers report on the vulnerabilities they discovered, where found and how the exploitation took place. The information obtained from this report will enable organizations make fixes to their software with a view to eliminating or mitigation the likelihood of successful illegal hacks (Heimdal Security, 2020).

HOW DO YOU BECOME AN ETHICAL HACKER?

Given the exponential rise in cyber-crime, ethical hacking is in high demand and many organizations will pay heftily for penetration testing. People, like Kevin Mitnick, became ethical hackers after operating as self-taught illegal hackers for long period. Others studied ethical hacking in formal educational institutions thereby becoming professionally certified ethical hacking. A good number of them nowadays who became ethical hackers learned this specialty through a combination of self-taught illegal hacking and formal certification programs (Heimdal security, 2020).

Below are three popular certification courses for becoming an ethical hacker:

*   Certified Ethical Hacker (CEH) from EC-Council
*   The Global Information Assurance Certification (GIAC) from the SANS Institute
*   The Offensive Security Certified Professional (OSCP) from Offensive Security

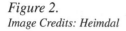

Figure 2.
Image Credits: Heimdal

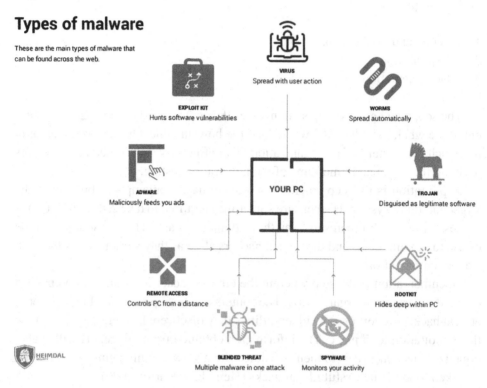

In addition to contracting penetration testers, some organizations offer bug bounty programs. A bug bounty program is an agreement between an organization and an ethical hacker wherein the organization agrees to offer another form of compensation

Figure 3.
Credits: CISCO Press: Breach of Confidentiality

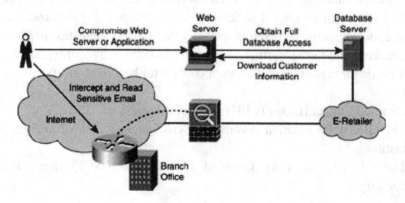

to white hat hackers who successfully identify and make known certain software bugs to the organization (Ethical Hacking and Measures, 2017).

Organizations that offer bug bounty programs are as follows: The United States Department of Defense, Microsoft, Salesforce, and IBM to name but a few.

Attackers can use many methods to compromise confidentiality, the most common of which are as follows:

ETHICAL HACKERS

See Figure 4.

Figure 4.

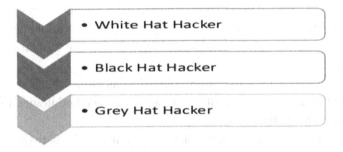

TYPES OF HACKERS AROUND THE GLOBE

Penetration Testing

Penetration testing is the assessment of the vulnerability or security of a system against various types of attacks that is performed by a security expert who has obtained initial permission. After obtaining permission, the tester will attempt to identify and exploit the system's vulnerabilities. The difference between a penetration test and an actual attack is that the former is done by a tester who has permission to do so and expose security weaknesses of the system. In addition, the tester is also given certain boundaries upon which to operate and perform the testing task (Cisco Press, 2013).

White, black, and grey represents the relationship between the hacker and the systems they are attacking.

'Black Hat' Hackers

The term "black hat" is believed to have originated from Western movies, wherein the bad guys wore black hats and the good guys wore white hats.

A black-hat hacker is an individual who attempts to gain unauthorized access into a system or network with a view to exploiting them for malicious purposes. The black-hat hacker does not have any permission or authority to compromise their intended targets. They try to wreak havoc by compromising security systems, modifying functions of websites and networks, or shutting down systems. They often do so with the intention of stealing or gaining access to passwords, financial information, and other personal details.

'White Hat' Hackers

White-hat hackers, on the other hand, are seen to be the good guys, working with organizations to help strengthen the security of a system. A white hat is permitted to engage the targets and to compromise them within the agreed upon rules of engagement.

White-hat hackers are most often referred to as ethical hackers. This person specializes in ethical hacking tools, techniques and methodologies to protect an organization's information systems.

Unlike black-hat hackers, ethical hackers exploit security networks and explore the paths to backdoors when they are legally allowed to do so. White-hat hackers always expose every vulnerability they can find in the organization's security system with the aim of fixing it before they can be exploited by malicious actors.

Some Fortune 50 companies like Facebook, Microsoft, and Google also use white-hat hackers.

'Grey Hat' Hackers

Like the Black Hats, Grey hats also exploit networks and computer systems, but do so without any malicious intent. They disclose all loopholes and vulnerabilities to law enforcement agencies and or intelligence agencies.

Grey-hat hackers do surf the net and hack into computer systems with the intent of notifying the administrator or the owner about the vulnerabilities that their system/ network may contain and to recommend immediate fixing. Grey hats may also extort the hacked victim, by offering to correct the defects in the system for a nominal fee.

There are many methods that attackers can use to compromise confidentiality. They include the following:

- **Ping sweeps and port scanning:** This entails searching a network host for open ports.
- **Packet sniffing:** The act of intercepting and logging traffic that passes over a digital network or some part of a network.
- **Emanations capturing:** Trying to deduce the organization's information by capturing the electrical transmissions from the equipment of the organization.
- **Overt channels:** Communications path within a computer system or network designed for the authorized transfer of data
- **Covert channels:** Concealed information within a transmission channel that is based on encoding data through the use of another set of events.
- **Wiretapping:** Tracking or eavesdropping the telephone or Internet conversations of a third party, often done secretly.
- **Social engineering:** The use of social skills or relationships to manipulate people inside the network to disclose or provide the information required to gain access to the network.
- **Dumpster diving:** Looking for information from company dumpsters or trash cans. Searching for information, such as phone books, organization charts, manuals, memos, charts, and other documentation that can be used by hackers.
- **Phishing:** Attempting to criminally obtain sensitive information, such as usernames and passwords, by sending messages purportedly from legitimate from trustworthy entities.
- **Pharming:** The act of redirecting the traffic of a website to another rogue website.

Many of these above-mentioned methods are used to compromise and attack confidentiality integrity and availability (CIA Triad) (Enisa, 2016).

Man-in-the-Middle Attacks

This is a complex form of IP spoofing. It is called man-in-the-middle attack, that is a form of attack wherein the hacker monitoring the traffic that comes across the network intercepts the communication as a secret intermediary between the sender and the receiver, as shown in the figure below.

Hackers use man-in-the-middle attacks to perform many security violations:

- The theft of information

Figure 5.
Credits: CISCO Press: IP Source Routing Attack

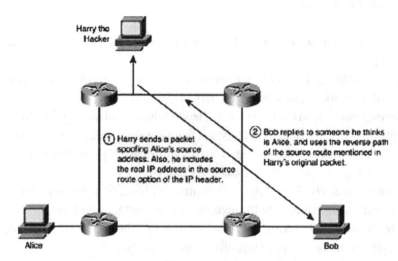

- The act of hijacking of a session with a view to gaining access to internal network resources
- Analysis of traffic to unlawfully obtain information about a network and its users
- DoS
- The intent and act of corrupting transmitted data
- The act of introducing new information into network sessions

The Characteristics of Social Engineering

- Pressure: Pressurizing the victim to do the bidding of the hacker is a way of expressing an urgency that would not allow the victim to think through what he or she is about to do.
- Time constraint: A malicious attacker will mislead you into thinking that you are missing out on an offer that will end soon or that an expiring account needs to be updated as soon as possible.
- Targeted manipulation: Seasoned hackers stalk and study the behavioral patterns, buying preferences and shopping locations and outlets, social media accounts to tailor-make scams that will successfully hit the intended targets (Imperva, 2019).

Methods of Social Engineering

- Phone calls: Criminals who pretend to represent a trusted organization, such as your bank, a familiar car dealership, would claim that you have a financial reward or monetary compensation for being a valued customer.
- Emails: You may receive an email with a phishing link luring you to a spoofed website that resembles your bank's for example or some other company that you are doing business with or receiving services from. You may unwitting or inadvertently a download a file, and in the process install malware on your computer (Imperva, 2019).
- Social media: Hackers may hack social media accounts of unsuspecting individuals and use those accounts to send out direct messages to lure other individuals to click links to "spoofed" websites.
- In-person: Some criminals may try to use your credentials to make an illegal entry your workplace.

DATA, VULNERABILITIES, AND COUNTERMEASURES

An attack on a computer system is a computer exploit, or an exploit. It usually takes of a weakness or vulnerability in the system. It may occur on an operating system, on an application or on a code.

A countermeasure is an action taken, a process implemented, a device, or system used that can help prevent and or mitigate the impacts of, threats or attacks (Johnston High School, 2020).

Key Concepts

An **asset** is a thing of value to an organization.

A **vulnerability** is a weakness in a system or its design that stands to be exploited by a threat agent. There is technically no risk associated with a vulnerability if there no threat toward that vulnerability.

A **threat** usually external, is a potential danger to information or systems.

A **risk** is the likelihood or probability that a certain vulnerability will be exploited.

An **exploit** is an attack performed against a vulnerability. It can be successful or unsuccessful.

A **countermeasure** is some form of a safeguard that is intended to protect and or mitigate the potential attack or threat.

PHASES OF AN ATTACK

Figure 6.

1. Reconnaissance

Reconnaissance is also known as 'foot-printing'. It is a technique for gathering information about a target or computer systems and or the organizational assets.

2. Scanning involves the probing of the computer system or the target to find vulnerabilities in them that can be exploited.

Scanning also involves the use of such tools as dialers, port scanners, network mappers, sweepers, and vulnerability scanners with a view to locating such information as computer names, IP addresses, and user accounts.

3. Gaining Access

Following the reconnaissance and scanning phases, vulnerabilities discovered are then exploited to gain access. The method of connection the hacker may use to exploit can be a local area network – LAN (either wired or wireless), local access to a PC, the Internet, or offline. Examples of gaining access would include stack based buffer overflows, denial of service (DoS), and session hijacking.

4.   Maintaining Access

Upon successful entry, hackers would in many cases want to maintain access for future exploitation and eventual attacks. In order to prevent would be hackers from taking advantage of the vulnerability, they may harden the system against other hackers or security personnel and give themselves exclusive access to the system with back-doors, root-kits, and Trojans.

5.   Covering Tacks

This phase involves the hacker destroying evidence or covering their tracks to avoid detection, to either continue using the system by removing or altering evidence like log files or intrusion detection systems (IDS) with a view to avoid legal action against them. Some activities during this phase include stenography, the use of tunneling protocols, and altering log files.

TYPES OF CYBER SECURITY ATTACKS

A **cyber-attack** is any and all types of offensive action that targeting computers, operating systems and or applications, infrastructures, computer networks or personal computer devices, accomplished through the use of various methods with the intent to steal, alter or destroy data or information systems. These can range from Phishing to denial of service (DOS) attacks and many others. This section below details the different types of cyber-attacks and related information.

Phishing Attack

Phishing attack is the use of technical trickery and social engineering wherein an attacker sends in an email which very much resembles one sent from a trusted source. The phishing attack is done for the purpose of gaining access to personal information of an individual. Usually done by persuading them or luring to click a link that will take the victim to a spoof website that looks very much like that of a legitimate organization like a bank or corporate entity. It will then send the data obtained to the attacker, where the user is redirected to another website housing the malware. Some emails may even contain malware attachments which upon

Figure 7.
Credits: assignmenthelp4me

downloading can infect the system and or reveal sensitive information that has been stored in the computer, thereby rendering it vulnerable

Spear phishing on the other hand is a very targeted type of phishing activity. Attackers methodically take the time to study the targets and create relevant, direct and personal messages. Since the end of February 2020 there is a huge increase of 667% in the cases of spear phishing attacks. This was detected by Barracuda Sentinel. In total 467,825 such attacks were detected out of which 9,116 are COVID-19 related. (Gartner, 2020).

Denial-of-Service (DoS) Attack and Distributed Denial-of-Service (DDoS) Attack

A denial-of-service attack occurs when the attacker continuously floods or bombards the server of victim with requests. The intent is to shut down the servers or keep them so busy that they cannot address the legitimate requests of the users. In some cases, when the load is too high, it might crash the servers as well.

Attackers using a DDoS attack in recent COVID-19 times, attempted to put out the website of the US Department of Health and Human Services (HHS) so they can deprive US citizens of information was being posted about the pandemic. However, the website continued to function appropriately albeit the little drop in performance. In the end it managed to serve the requests under increased load.

Vishing Attack

This is form of phishing attack in which the attacker makes use of a phone to contact the customer to trick them into getting their personal details by claiming to be a legitimate user, like bank insurance officers in order to get the bank details of the user. The attacker uses bogus strategies to deceive the client to get the details from them. Viruses

Virus

Viruses are the malware programs containing malicious code intended to disrupt the normal working of computer systems. Viruses can create replicas throughout the systems of the user for further infection. It can also attach itself to the file of another computer and thereby spread itself. In addition to corrupting a user's file like bank account details; it then goes on to steal all the information contained in the file.

Malware Attack

The use of malicious code is at the center of malware attack. It can destroy the whole network including the server and its clients. It provides access to sensitive information which is what the hackers need to take control over the computer system. The danger it poses is that untraced in the network for prolonged durations and in the long run sniff data from the packets, thereby wreaking havoc by leaking information. It sometimes resembles a legitimate code with the propensity to self-propagates through the network, thus spreading to all connected devices in the network.

On April 20, 2020, an IT firm in the US was attacked by Maze ransomware which encrypted all their data and sent out emails containing an IP address and a file to the customers. It locked the entire organization out of their systems and then proceeded to encrypt the data. It also stole the organization's data, thereby compromising the privacy of customers. The organization ended up paying demanded ransom to get its data decrypted and gain and regaining lost access (Trendmicro, 2020).

SQL Injection Attack

As the name implies, SQL injection is an attack on database-based webget sites. Upon a successful attack such sensitive information as login credentials, payment information and personal information of clients will be made available to the attacker. This attack is usually carried out using the SQL commands. They are inserted into the database to run certain operations.

In 2016, a SQL Injection attack was carried off at the Illinois Board of Elections which compromised the data of 200,000 citizens. This resulted in the server being taken down for 10 consecutive days for the purpose of repairing the server and fixing the flaws and vulnerabilities.

Man-in-the-Middle Attack

It is a form breach wherein an attacker eavesdrops the packet transfer taking place between a client and a server. This enables an attacker to gain access to certain sensitive information. The attacker can also capture and modify the packet before sending it to its destination.

A logistics organization from Mumbai, India fell prey to an unidentified attacker and allegedly lost $16,000. The attacker used MITM technique to sniff the payment the company was about to receive, by hacking their official account (Youth Incorporated, 2020).

Password Attacks

These are hacking attempts by hackers to gain unauthorized access to the organizational security system. In order to gain access, the hackers may utilize some password cracking or security tools. These password cracking tools are mostly used in the login procedures with the objective of getting an unauthentic pass to the user's account or stealing the user's credential to name but a few.

Brute Force Attack

Brute force attack is a networking attack in which the attacker tries to gain access to the system by force i.e. trying all the possible methods and password combinations of illegal characters, numerals, letters and or alphanumeric guesses. The procedure is carried out until a correct access code or key is found.

TaoBao, a venture of Alibaba Group was successfully attacked and fell prey to a massive brute force attack, which led to breach of up to 21 million accounts. The attackers were believed to have used a database of 99 million accounts.

Spyware and Keyloggers

As the name implies, spyware is a kind of malware attack that aims at identifying the activities of a victim of their computer system. A Keyloggers on the other hand aims at recording all the keystrokes pressed by victims. Basically, these spywares and Keyloggers work when the victim installs or downloads any corrupted file from malicious websites. In the end this sensitive and crucial information together with the user's browser history are shared with the malicious hacker who controls all this activity at his end.

Cross-Site Scripting (XOS)

This attack is an injection breach, in which websites are used as hosts and malicious scripts are sent through them, given the trust people usually have for their content. This breach is accomplished by attaching the malicious code with the dynamic content of the website. The target browser which executes JavaScript code snippets are sent to the victim's browser.

In 2018, British Airways suffered a data breach which involved a cross-site scripting attack. It affected almost 380,000 booking transactions between August and September of that year. The breach impacted mobile apps and website users. (assignmenthelp4me, 2021)

REASONS FOR RISE IN CYBERCRIME

It is difficult to obtain accurate numbers detailing the steady increase of cybercrime throughout the globe as the statistics are built on numbers of attacks, breaches, and other security events that are reported, leaving unreported numbers unaccounted for. However, CNN Money cites a report by Ponemon Institute that claims 47% of adults in the United States alone have had their personal information exposed, with 110 million of these data breaches occurring over a 12-month period from May 2013 to May 2014 (as cited in Pagliery, 2014). A world statistics portal reports that two of the most well-known companies suffering data breaches, Adobe and eBay, had 152 million and 145 million records stolen as of August 2015 (Statista, 2015). There are two major reasons for this rise in cybercrime over the last decade: the low risk and relative safety for attackers; and the increasing targets of opportunity provided by the Internet.

THE ECONOMIC IMPACT OF CYBER-ATTACKS

Cybersecurity Ventures anticipate a steep rise of global cybercrime costs to grow by 15 percent per year over the next five years, reaching $10.5 trillion USD per annum by 2025, up from $3 trillion USD in 2015. The estimated damage cost is based on historical cybercrime figures which include annual increase in organized crime, gang hacking activities, and a cyberattack surface which will be an order of a magnitude greater in 2025 than it is today.

Cybercrime costs can be measured in terms of damage and destruction of data, stolen money, loss in productivity, theft of intellectual property, stolen personal and financial data, embezzlement, fraud, forensic investigation, alteration and deletion of hacked data and systems, and reputational harm. In its report "The Economic Impact of Cyberattacks on Municipalities", KnowBe4 stated that in ransomware attacks, the ransom paid per event in municipalities from 2017 to 2020 was $125,6971. Ransomware attacks are known to cause significant downtime and denial of critical services in the community, such as healthcare and law enforcement. The analysis shows that the average downtime resulting from a ransomware attack is 9.6 days.

CONCLUSION

In the conclusion phase, the ethical hacker is expected to craft a detailed documentation or report for the organization or client that hired him or her. The report will contain an analysis of the vulnerabilities, possibilities and impact of hacking. The vulnerabilities detected will be explained in detail and recommendations put forward to address any and all security solutions (EC Council, ethical hacker, 2017).

The report will be in the form an executive summary with results obtained from the reconnaissance and scanning stages, with particular emphasis to those indicating possible areas of weakness.

The recommendations will detail actions to be taken to ensure closing down any weaknesses or vulnerabilities. This report is done with the aim of creating a clear sequence of events or audit trail between each stage. That was, a reader will be able to follow on what was asked for, what was has been tested and why, its results as well as the recommendations that have been put forward by the tester.

REFERENCES

Assignment help - high QUALITY Assignment help in Australia. (2019). Retrieved March 27, 2021, from https://assignmenthelp4me.com/

Certified ethical hacker: InfoSec cyber Security Certification: EC-Council. (2016). Retrieved March 27, 2021, from https://www.eccouncil.org/

Cisco Press. (2013). Retrieved March 27, 2021, from https://www.ciscopress.com/articles/article.asp?p=1998559

Course Overview. (2020). *Johnstone High School – Computing and Junior Education.* Retrieved March 27, 2021, from http://cybersecurity.jhigh.co.uk/index.html

Enisa. (2016). *Vulnerabilities and Exploits.* Retrieved March 24, 2021 https://www.enisa.europa.eu/topics/csirts-in-europe/glossary/vulnerabilities-and-exploits

Ethical hacking and countermeasures. (2017). Cengage Learning.

Gartner Inc. (2021). *Fueling the future of business.* Retrieved March 27, 2021, from https://www.gartner.com/en

Grimes, R. (2019, February 27). *What is ethical hacking? How to get paid to break into computers.* Retrieved March 27, 2021, from https://www.csoonline.com/article/3238128/what-is-ethical-hacking-and-how-to-become-an-ethical-hacker.html

Heimdal Security - Proactive Cyber Security Software. (n.d.). Retrieved March 28, 2021, from https://heimdalsecurity.com/en/

Maze ransomware Attacks Us It Firm. (2020). Retrieved March 28, 2021, from https://www.trendmicro.com/vinfo/us/security/news/cybercrime-and-digital-threats/maze-ransomware-attacks-us-it-firm

Netwrix. (2021). *Powerful data security made easy.* Retrieved March 27, 2021, from https://www.netwrix.com/

Pagliery, J. (2014). *Bitcoin: And the Future of Money.* Academic Press.

Statista. (2015, August). *Number of compromised data records in selected data breaches as of August 2015.* Retrieved from https://www.statista.com/statistics/290525/cyber-crime-biggest-online-data-breaches-worldwide/

Surge in Cyberattacks Leaves Economic Impact on U.S. State and Local Governments By CISOMAG. (2020). https://cisomag.eccouncil.org/magazine/

Webopedia. (2021). *What is Social Engineering?* Retrieved March 24, 2021 https://www.webopedia.com/definitions/social-engineering/

What Is Social Engineering: Attack Techniques & Prevention Methods: Imperva. (2019, December 29). Retrieved March 28, 2021, from https://www.imperva.com/learn/application-security/social-engineering-attack/

Youth Incorporated Magazine. (2020). *Ethical Hacking: A New Age IT Career For You*. Retrieved March 24, 2021 https://youthincmag.com/ethical-hacking-a-new-age-it-career-

Chapter 2
Cybersecurity Risks, Vulnerabilities, and Countermeasures to Prevent Social Engineering Attacks

Nabie Y. Conteh
Southern University at New Orleans, USA

Paul J. Schmick
University of Maryland Global Campus, USA

ABSTRACT

The broad objective of this study is to evaluate the vulnerabilities of an organization's information technology infrastructure, which include hardware and software systems, transmission media, local area networks, wide area networks, enterprise networks, intranets, and its use of the internet to cyber intrusions. To achieve this objective, the chapter explains the importance of social engineering in network intrusions and cyber-theft and the reasons for the rapid expansion of cybercrime. The chapter also includes a complete description and definition of social engineering, the role it plays in network intrusion and cyber identity theft, a discussion of the reasons for the rise in cybercrimes, and their impact on organizations. In closing the authors recommend some preventive measures and possible solutions to the threats and vulnerabilities of social engineering. The chapter concludes that while technology has a role to play in reducing the impact of social engineering attacks, the vulnerability resides with human behavior, human impulses, and psychological predispositions.

DOI: 10.4018/978-1-7998-6504-9.ch002

INTRODUCTION

Social engineering, also known as human hacking, is the art of tricking employees and consumers into disclosing their credentials and then using them to gain access to networks or accounts. It is a hacker's tricky use of deception or manipulation of people's tendency to trust, be corporative, or simply follow their desire to explore and be curious. Sophisticated IT security systems cannot protect systems from hackers or defend against what seems to be authorized access. People are easily hacked, making them and their social media posts high-risk attack targets. It is often easy to get computer users to infect their corporate network or mobiles by luring them to spoof websites and or tricking them into clicking on harmful links and or downloading and installing malicious applications and or backdoors.

In a 2013 study conducted by TNS Global for Halon an e-mail security service, 30 percent of the surveyed populace comprised of 1,000 adults in the U.S. disclosed that they would open an e-mail even if they were aware it contained a virus or was suspicious (Ragan, 2013). Even with robust campaigns conveying the dangers of opening suspicious e-mails a large majority of e-mail users remain vulnerable to social engineering attacks (Mann & Sharma, 2012). *To confront the challenges posed from social engineering attacks, recommendations deriving from research offer options to reduce the probability of success from a social engineering attack.*

With cyber security incidents growing exponentially in terms of frequency and damage to an organizations reputation in their respective marketplace, users and organizations have not adequately deployed defenses to discourage would-be attacker's intent to strike. The terms *information and network security* continue to dominate U.S. headlines with a large-scale cyberattack surpassing the probability of a physical terrorist attack on U.S. soil. In fact, in a 2013 interview of FBI Director James Comey, the Director testified before a Senate Homeland Security Committee that cyber-attacks have surpassed terrorism as a major domestic threat, with the threat continuing to rise (Anonymous, 2013).

In this paper social engineering is defined along with the types of social engineering attacks. In addition, this research will identify why cyber theft continues to advance at an alarming rate. Furthermore, psychological variables that contribute to vulnerabilities will be discussed. And finally, studies will be presented that identify key considerations regarding social engineering testing and training, and point to how users can be coached to prevent attacks which offers a promising methodology to reduce system and user risk.

What Is Social Engineering?

Engebretson (2011) defines social engineering as "one of the more simple methods to gather information about a target through the process of exploiting human weakness that is inherit to every organization." The foundation of an attack is to persuade the forfeiture of information that is confidential then exploit an individual or an organization. In essence, an attacker engages social engineering as a tactic to use human insiders and information to circumvent computer security solutions through deceit.

Regarding the human vulnerability of social engineering Luo, Brody, Seazzu, & Burd (2011) note that while social engineering is identified as a low-tech attack; the attack aims at manipulating victims to divulge confidential information and is successful in its attempt due to exploiting personality vulnerabilities. Social engineering as a tactic deploys techniques to gain access to private and confidential information by exploiting flaws in human logic know as cognitive biases (Luo, et al., 2011). While security technology measures aim at improving information system security, human factors represent a weak-link which is exploited during a social engineering attack.

Bisson (2015) notes that social engineering is "a term that encompasses a broad spectrum of malicious activity" and identifies *five* of the most common types of social engineering attacks to target victims which include:

1. Phishing

Phishing scams attempt to obtain personal information such as names, addresses and other personal identifiable information (PII) such as social security numbers. Phishing scams may embed links to redirect users to suspicious websites that appear legitimate. These types of scams create a sense of urgency to manipulate users to act in a manner that challenges good judgment.

2. Pretexting

This type of social engineering attack is driven by a fabrication scenario attempting to confirm and steal personal information from a target. Advanced attacks attempt to exploit a weakness of an organization or company. This method requires the attacker to build a credible story that leaves little room to question doubt by a target. The strategy is to use fear and urgency while building a sense of trust with a victim to confirm or obtain sought information.

3. Baiting

Baiting is similar to a phishing attack but lures a victim through enticement strategies. Hackers use the lure of promised goods if a user surrenders log-in credentials to a specific site. Baiting schemes are not limited to digital on-line schemes and can also be launched through the use of physical media.

4.   Quid Pro Quo

Similar to Baiting, but this type of threat is presented as a technical service in exchange for information. A common threat is for an attacker to impersonate an information technology representative and offer assistance to a victim who may be experiencing technical challenges. The attacker aims to launch malware on a user's system.

5.   Tailgating

This type of attack uses tailgating and piggybacking to gain access to restricted areas. This attack exposes those who have an ability to grant or gain access to a restricted area by an attacker who may impersonate delivery personnel or others who may require temporary access.

Social Engineering and Its Role in Cyber-Theft

Information Security is defined as *"protecting information and information systems from unauthorized access, use, disclosure, disruption, modification, or destruction"* according to U.S. law (Andress, 2011). And while so much attention in terms of resources and training to overcome information security breaches have been deployed, Nakashima and Peterson (2014) note the Center for Strategic and International Studies identifies the annual cost of cybercrime and economic espionage to cost to global economy more than $445 billion annually – or almost *one* percent of total global income (Strohm, 2014).

Hackers are getting increasingly sophisticated and adept at their social engineering attacks. They are able to piece together disparate data from various sources and namely, social media, corporate blogs, and data and to painstakingly pull crucial and key data from well-meaning employees which these cyber-criminals use to attack networks and steal invaluable data and even hold corporations hostage and in some cases damage the object of their targets.

Regarding the rise of cybercrime and theft, Grimes (2014) identifies key indicators as to the rise and cause of cybercrime which financially impacts both individuals and organizations. One reason for cyber theft appeal is the benefit of theft by ambiguity. Internet crimes are committed by thousands of cybercriminals world-wide but few are prosecuted and jailed. In addition, cybercriminals do not have to be intelligent to be successful in digital theft, but are willing to take risks because of the benefits of distance from a victim while taking little risk and little exposure.

Many cyber thefts take place globally and law enforcement agencies are limited in the jurisdictional boundaries to pursue cybercriminals. The pursuit also includes working with other law enforcement agencies outside of domestic jurisdictions. While this is less complex domestically, getting international support to pursue international theft remains a challenge for U.S. Law enforcement. In essence, most international governments do not cooperate with each other (Taylor et al., 2015).

Evidence plays another factor and a lack of successful convictions are due to a lack of evidence that can be delivered in court to prosecute cyber criminals. Two primary variables relate to evidence fulfillment such as obtaining evidence that is credible to hold individuals accountable. Second, few organizations have the legal expertise to prepare legal evidence in cybercrime cases which takes planning, commitment and resources. These challenges lower the probability that a criminal even if caught will be prosecuted and jailed.

To overcome crime in the cyber domain, a lack of resources is perhaps the leading contributor to its exponential growth. Few organizations have the dedicated resources to pursue internet crimes and criminals. The challenge of pursuing cyber theft is costly and without a potential return-on-investment (ROI) dedicated resources are difficult to justify.

While the cost of cyber victimization is nearly a half trillion dollars, it has not hurt global economies and may even be in the realm of appearing as a cost of doing business. For meaningful change to occur, once cybercrime hurts individuals and organizations to an unbearable point, the reality or managing risk and loss have been built into the fabric of organizations, and individual victimization from small-scale occurrences have become noise that is expected.

Psychological Variables and Contribution to Cybercrimes

Social engineering attacks challenge information security professionals because no technical countermeasures to-date can eliminate the human vulnerability (Luo, Brody, Seazzu, & Burd, 2011). Identifying the cues of human error and successful social engineering attacks Luo, et al. (2011) argues the social psychology influences of *"alternative routes to persuasion, attitudes and beliefs that affect human interactions, and techniques for persuasion influence"* expose the psychological vulnerabilities that enable a successful social engineering attack.

To seek foundations of the interest to open potentially damaging e-mails, Ragan (2013) notes the diversity of intent to engage in such behavior is specific among genders with women enticed to open malicious e-mails appearing from social networks, while men fall prey to e-mails communicating power, money and sex. Because social engineering attacks tap into human psychological impulses reducing engagement remains a challenge because occurrences aim at human psychological vulnerabilities (Vacca, 2013).

Further evaluating the social psychological influences, alternate routes to persuasion contribute to successful social engineering attacks through influencing a victim's emotions towards fear or excitement which may alter a responsible action. Regarding attitudes and beliefs, this refers to the differences concerning the beliefs between the victim and his/her social engineering attackers. And lastly, influencing techniques rely on peripheral paths to persuasion that influence behavior and action (Luo et al., 2011).

Because of the emotional exposure and triggered response initiated by social engineering attacks, without awareness of the vulnerabilities revealed by artful exposure of human susceptibility to engage in the process, denying an attackers ploy is a challenge. However, studies demonstrate awareness through corporate education campaigns may provide a virtual barrier to reduce the success rate of social engineering attacks. In totality, the chief strategy may reside in awareness in the manipulation tactics to obtain valuable and confidential information to prevent social engineering attackers' from acquiring information to exploit a user or organization.

Social Engineering Techniques – Human and Technical

Luo et al. (2011) identifies several human or technical means that social engineering attackers can deploy from phishing to dumpster diving as tactics to gain visibility or obtain confidential information. For aggressive and successful attackers a synergy of human and technical strategy may be deployed to obtain ample information on an individual or to gain access to an organization. Regarding the steps of gathering

Figure 1. Four Steps of Social Engineering
(Luo et al., 2011)

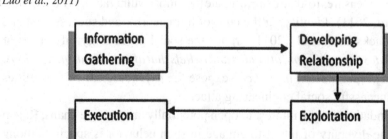

information through execution of a social engineering attack Luo et al. (2011) identify the steps in the attack process.

Figure 1 above graphically explains the stepwise approaches in the execution of social engineering attacks. The process begins with the first phase of studying and gathering information, then a relationship is established. In the exploitation phase, access into the system is gained and in the final phase, the attacked is implemented.

Social engineering attacks can be categorized in either human or technology deployments. Direct human engagement stems from an attacker who has obtained personal information about a victim and develops a relationship with the user. Because the attacker deploys a strategy of a known or trusted party, the victim becomes susceptible and exploited, and relinquishes sensitive or personal company information; therefore contributing to the pieces of the puzzle the attacker can use to his/her advantage.

Technical attacks are more unambiguous and deployed through a host of options such as; software programs, e-mail attachments, pop-up windows and websites (Luo et al., 2011). Perhaps the most successful technical ploy to draw a user into divulging account usernames and passwords by prompting victims to input user and password information in pop-up windows. Websites and pop-up windows can appear as a site frequently visited by a user, however, the script-embedded pop-up window manipulates the user to enter a username and password which delivers the information to the attacker.

Preventive Measures Against Social Engineering

It is evident that regardless of how technologically secure a network seems the human element will always be a vulnerability. The success rate and number of cybercrimes are steadily on the rise due to the level of anonymity social engineering offers malicious actors. Businesses have to remain cognitive of the various threat actors and their plethora of attacks so they are able to respond accordingly. There are technical and non-technical safeguards that can be implemented to lower the risk associated with social engineering to a tolerable level. Companies are adding multiple layers to their security schemes so that if the mechanism in the outer layer fails, a mechanism in at least one inner layer can help prevent a threat from turning into a disaster (Risk Mitigation). This concept is known as Multi-Layer Defense or Defense in Depth. A good Defense in Depth structure includes a mixture of the following precautionary measures:

- **Security Policy:** A well written policy should include technical and nontechnical approaches that are downward driven by executive management. Every organization should integrate security into their operational objectives.

- **Education and Training:** Employees ought to be required to attend initial training during orientation and recurring refresher trainings. This builds awareness by exposing users to commonly employed tactics and behaviors targeted by a social engineer.
- **Network Guidance:** The organization have to safeguard the network by whitelisting authorized websites, using Network address translation (NAT), and disabling unused applications and ports. Network users have to maintain complex passwords that are changed every 60 days.
- **Audits and Compliance:** Organizations have to actively verify that their security policy is being adhered to. Some detective controls include reviewing network logs, re-validating employees' permissions, and checking desktop configurations at least bi-monthly.
- **Technical Procedures:** The network should have multiple layers of defense to protect data and core infrastructure. Software like Intrusion Prevention Systems (IPS), Intrusion Detection Systems (IDS) and firewalls should be installed on every device. Demilitarized Zones (DMZ), web filters and Virtual Private Network (VPN) should be installed on all external facing services.
- **Physical Guidance:** There are a range of options that can be implemented to protect physical assets. Using a combination of security guards, mantraps and security cameras to deter intruders from entering the premises is beneficial. In places where physical hardware is located businesses should employ multifactor authentication, biometrics or access control list before access is granted.

To overcome the challenges of social engineering attacks Luo et al. (2011) identify the necessity of a multidimensional approach to overcome threats through a holistic approach of addressing organizational policies, procedures, standards, employee training and awareness programs, and incident response. While all areas to combat this threat are critical, without employee training expensive infrastructure and network security investment means little considering only seven percent of U.S. organizations deploy training programs and materials in phishing education (Diana, 2015).

Evaluating variables of cause and identifying those who are susceptible in an organization Chitery, Singh, Bag, & Singh (2012) identify the drivers, targets and motivation behind social engineering attacks. The 2012 study attempted to demonstrate an analytical approach towards social engineering attacks and identify attacker trends. The study which surveyed an undisclosed amount of IT professionals sheds light on potential training measures for organizations that are eager to deploy information security awareness programs to reduce the risk of employee proneness to a social engineering attack.

Figure 2. Questionnaire Results Regarding the Motivation Behind Social Engineering Attacks

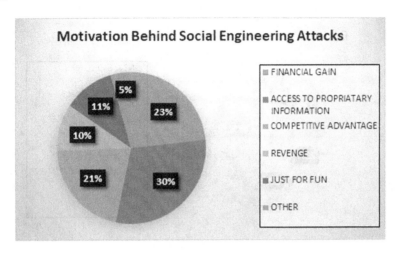

According to a study conducted by Chitery, Singh, Bag, & Singh (2012) as introduced in the preceding paragraph above, figure 2 depicts the motivating factors behind social engineering attacks. It is evident that the access motivated by the need to gain proprietary information ranks the highest in terms of the volume which is 30%. Financial gain ranks second, followed by the need for competitive advantage, then by "just for fun", revenge and last and least by unnamed others. Figure 3 depicts the results from the same study as above obtained on entities that are vulnerable to social engineering attacks. The most vulnerable group is the new employees (41%), followed by clients and customers (23%), then by IT professionals (17%), by Partners and Contractors (12%) and lastly followed by others.

In another study by Bowen, Devarajan & Stolfo (2011) this Columbia University study measured enterprise susceptibility to phishing attacks which is a technical path and deployment mechanism to instigate a social engineering attack. The 2011 study's primary focus conducted by Columbia University was on reinforced training and the impact to prevent social engineering attacks. As the results show in tables 1 and 2 below, the study tested user vulnerabilities using decoy e-mails to lure users to supply information or access phony e-mails so data could be gathered and utilized for training purposes to prevent future attacks.

The Bowen, et al. (2011) study was conducted by deploying two rounds of experiments. Users were probed repeatedly, then educated each time to understand how the luring techniques occurred until victims stopped falling prey to attacks. The data ultimately supports that both repetitious probes followed by education offers

Figure 3. Questionnaire Results Regarding Entities Which Present Risk of Falling Prey to a Social Engineering Attack

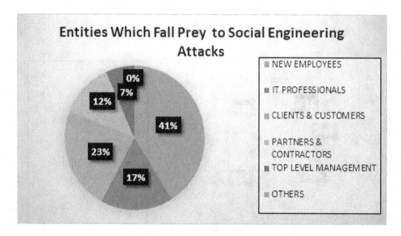

value and a return on investment (ROI) to limit successful probes of users regardless of psychological predispositions or gender.

Evaluating the data from both rounds of the Columbia University experiment confirms users can be coached to deploy caution before opening suspicious e-mail messages. As the data supports, by reaffirming threats through repetitive

Table 1. The Number of Responses for Each Round for the First Experiment to Measure the User Response to Phony Phish

Decoy Type	1ˢᵗ Round	2ⁿᵈ Round	3ʳᵈ Round	4ᵗʰ Round
Email with internal URLs	52	2	0	NA
Email with external URLs	177	15	1	0
Forms to obtain credentials[2]	39/20	4/1	0	NA
Beacon Documents	45	0	NA	NA

Table 2. The Number of Responses for Each Round for the Second Experiment to Measure the User Response to Phony Phish

Decoy Type	1ˢᵗ Round	2ⁿᵈ Round	3ʳᵈ Round	4ᵗʰ Round
Email with internal URLs	69	7	1	0
Email with external URLs	176	10	3	0
Forms to obtain credentials	69/50	10/9	0	NA
Beacon Documents	71	2	0	NA

communication, although slower learners had the highest probability that they would fall-prey to social engineering attacks, users were still able to be coached to disengage in the luring process of social engineering attacks.

Limitations of the Study

Luo et al. (2011) recognizes key considerations that can be learned from social engineering penetration testing and education. Most importantly, the 2011 Columbia University study noted in this research paper identifies that education followed by additional social engineering testing leads to a dramatic reduction in social engineering attack success, therefore reducing information system and network vulnerability. However, the 2011 Columbia University study offers no consideration to how frequently testing and training may be required to maintain the same results. In essence, the limitations of the Columbia University study prevents drawing an absolute conclusion that the same results should be expected if future testing was conducted. This leaves consideration to the deployment of recurrent training models after periods of time to determine if similar results can be produced by users after one phase of testing to determine if training efforts are lasting.

CONCLUSION

To overcome cyber security incidents involving social engineering attacks, research supports the most effective defense is an educated computer user. To consider is those most vulnerable which are identified in this research as new employees within an organization, as specifically shown in figure 3 above, with the attacker seeking personal identifiable information (PII) from those engaged. Further supported in this research are the psychological variables that contribute to user vulnerability. *This paper concludes that while technology has a role to play in reducing the impact of social engineering attacks, the vulnerability resides with human behavior, human impulses and psychological predispositions that can be influenced through education. Ultimately, investment in organizational education campaigns offer optimism that social engineering attacks can be reduced, but an absolute solution to overcome such cybersecurity threats has yet to be put-forward.*

REFERENCES

Andress, J. (2011). *The Basics of Information Security*. Elsevier.

Anonymous. (2013). *FBI: Cyber-attacks surpassing terrorism as major domestic threat*. Retrieved from https://www.rt.com/usa/fbi-cyber-attack-threat-739/

Bisson, D. (2015, Mar 23). 5 Social Engineering Attacks to Watch Out For. *The State of Security*. Retrieved from https://www.tripwire.com/state-of-security/security-awareness/5-social-engineering-attacks-to-watch-out-for/

Bowen, B. M., Devarajan, R., & Stolfo, S. (2011). Measuring the Human Factor of Cyber Security. *Columbia University*. Retrieved from http://www.cs.columbia.edu/~bmbowen/papers/metrics_hst.pdf

Chitery. A., Singh, D., Bag, M., & Singh, V. (2012). A Comprehensive Study of Social Engineering Based Attacks in India to Develop a Conceptual Model. *International Journal of Information & Network Security, 1*(2), 45-53.

Diana, A. (2015, May 19). *Social Engineering Targets Weakest Security Link: Employees*. Retrieved from http://www.enterprisetech.com/2015/05/19/social-engineering-targets-weakest-security-link-employees/

Engebretson, P. (2011). *The Basics of Hacking and Penetration Testing*. Elsevier.

Grimes, R. A. (2015). 5 Reasons Internet Crime is Worse Than Ever. *Info World*. Retrieved From https://www.infoworld.com/article/2608631/security/5-reasons-internet-crime-is-worse-than-ever.html?page=2

Luo, X., Brody, R., Seazzu, A., & Burd, S. (2011). Social Engineering: The Neglected Human Factor for Information Security Management. *Information Resources Management Journal, 24*(3), 1–8.

Mann, P. S., & Sharma, M. (2012). Social Engineering: A Partial Technical Attack. *IJCSI International Journal of Computer Science Issues, 9*(2), 557-559. Retrieved from http://citeseerx.ist.psu.edu/viewdoc/download?doi=10.1.1.401.7920&rep=rep1&type=pdf

Nakashima, E., & Peterson, A. (2014, June 9). Report: Cybercrime and espionage costs $445 billion annually. *The Washington Post*. Retrieved from https://www.washingtonpost.com/world/national-security/report-cybercrime-and-espionage-costs-445-billion-annually/2014/06/08/8995291c-ecce-11e3-9f5c-9075d5508f0a_story.html

Ragan, S. (2013). Social Engineering: Study finds Americans willingly open malicious emails. *CSO*. Retrieved from https://www.csoonline.com/article/2133877/social-engineering/social-engineering--study-finds-americans-willingly-open-malicious-emails.html

Strohm, C. (2014). Cyber Theft, Already a 445 Billion Business, to Grow Bigger. *Insurance Journal*. Retrieved https://www.insurancejournal.com/news/national/2014/06/09/331333.htm

Taylor, R. W., Fritsch, E. J., & Liederbach, J. (2015). *Digital Crime and Digital Terrorism* (3rd ed.). Pearson Education.

Vacca, J. R. (2013). *Computer and Information Security* (2nd ed.). Kaufmann.

Chapter 3

The Unprecedented Rise in Cybercrime and the Role of the Human Vulnerability Factor

Nabie Y. Conteh
Southern University at New Orleans, USA

Malcolm D. Royer
University of Maryland Global Campus, USA

ABSTRACT

This chapter is primarily intended to firstly define and review the literature in cybersecurity and vividly shed light on the mechanisms involved in the social engineering phenomenon. It will discuss the various attempts at network intrusion and the steps typically taken in the implementation of cyber-thefts. The chapter will provide the rationale behind the justification of why humans are considered to be the weakest link in these attacks. The study will also explain the reasons for the rise in cybercrimes and their impact on organizations. In closing, the chapter will put forward some recommendations to serve as preventative measures and solutions to the threats and vulnerabilities posed by cyber-attacks. Finally, measures, such as conducting regular, thorough, and relevant awareness training, frequent drills, and realistic tests, will be addressed with a view to maintaining a steady focus on the overall discipline of the organization, thereby hardening the component of the network that is the softest by nature—the human vulnerability factor.

DOI: 10.4018/978-1-7998-6504-9.ch003

1. INTRODUCTION

The security of an organization is only as strong as its weakest component. In an era of increasing technological advances in the methods of conducting business, one might think that the security of those resources mostly lies in technical controls and programming algorithms. While the technical side of security is critically important, there is a vulnerability that cannot be removed by technological means. That vulnerability is unique to a particular element unavoidably necessary in the daily operation of any company. This indispensable component is the human employee, who is susceptible to attacks of a decidedly low-tech nature—social engineering.

2. SOCIAL ENGINEERING

2.1 Definition

The term "social engineering" as it pertains to computer and network security is not new—it has been around since at least 1995 when Al Berg used it in his article "Cracking a Social Engineer" in LAN Times—but it has not yet made its way into all standard dictionaries. The 2015 editions of the Merriam-Webster, Random House, and Cambridge Free English dictionaries only define social engineering in terms of the social or political sciences, not security. Among the information security community, however, social engineering refers to "the practice of fooling someone into giving up something they wouldn't otherwise surrender through the use of psychological tricks" (Vacca & Curry, 2013). Curry goes on to state that social engineers "rely on the normal behavior of people presented with data or a social situation to respond in a predictable, human way" and explains that this kind of attack relies on "presenting trusted logos and a context that seems normal but is in fact designed to create a vulnerability that the social engineer can exploit" (Vacca & Curry, 2013).

In his book *Ghost in the Wires* about his exploits as a hacker, Kevin Mitnick defines social engineering as "the casual or calculated manipulation of people to influence them to do things they would not ordinarily do" (Mitnick & Simon, 2011). He gives a clear example of a typical method of obtaining unauthorized information as a part of his breaking into U.S. Leasing's computer network:

I would call the company I'd targeted, ask for their computer room, make sure I was talking to a system administrator, and tell him, "This is [whatever fictitious name popped into my head at that moment], from DEC support. We've discovered a catastrophic bug in your version of RSTS/E. You could lose data." This is a very powerful social-engineering technique, because the fear of losing data is so great that most people won't hesitate to cooperate. (Mitnick & Simon, 2011)

Accurate as this example is, it only depicts one aspect of social engineering: pretexting—setting the conditions (a story, subtle or explicit clues, name-dropping, internal buzz-words and terminology, etc.) for a victim to believe that the attacker comes from a legitimate background. The other forms of attack that fall under the classification of social engineering, including the definitions pit forward in this article are:

- Baiting—leaving Trojan horse style equipment or software lying in the open with an enticing title or appearance as bait.
- Phishing—using a scam email to deceive a victim.
- Piggybacking (or tailgating)—following someone into a secure environment, with or without them detection.
- Quid Pro Quo—giving someone something in return; exploiting a person's goodwill.
- Shoulder Surfing—watching someone enter knowledge-based credentials and remembering them for future unauthorized use.
- Vishing—using an interactive voice response system to trick a victim into inputting personal information over the phone.

According to (Granger, 2010), regardless of the specific attack method, the basic methods of persuasion used are "impersonation, ingratiation, conformity, diffusion of responsibility, and plain old friendliness….the main objective is to convince the person disclosing the information that the social engineer is in fact a person that they can trust" (Granger, 2010). An additional supplement to the information-gathering process and development of a plausible background prior to pretexting is dumpster diving—sifting through discarded files for sensitive information.

3. ROLE IN NETWORK INTRUSION AND CYBER THEFT

Social engineering plays a major and enduring role in network intrusion and cyber theft. This is not to say that it is an absolutely necessary role, as a cracker could conceivably infiltrate a system without any human interaction through exploiting technical vulnerabilities. The significance of the role that it plays is due to the ongoing vulnerability any system has and will continue to have—its users and administrators.

3.1 Humans Are the Weakest Link

Because people are involved in the management and use of any computer network, they will always have to be considered one of the links to the security chain. This link is and will continue to be the weakest for the simple reason that people are easy to manipulate. We are subject to emotions that frequently override any commitment to logic that we may have. We have a psychological dimension that computers, which are based upon pure, straightforward logic, do not have. Our psychological weaknesses and needs, coupled with our faulty memory and flighty attention span, leave us highly vulnerable to deception and emotional manipulation.

Dr. George Simon talks about successful psychological manipulation in his book *In Sheep's Clothing*, stating that it requires the manipulator to conceal aggressive intentions and behaviors, know the psychological vulnerabilities of the victim, and be ruthless enough to disregard any harm caused to the victim (Simon, 2010). Since there is no psychological aspect to a computer's processing and intentions and behaviors are perceived in terms of analysis of a sequence of actions taken, these approaches would be irrelevant to a technical system were it not for the human component. According to Dr. Harriet Braiker in her book *Who's Pulling Your Strings?*, manipulators control their victims using positive and negative reinforcement, intermittent or partial reinforcement, punishment, and traumatic one-trial learning (Braiker, 2004). They play upon the desires that most people have for affirmation, affection, and appreciation while taking advantage of our natural tendency to want to help others, especially those who share an affiliation of some sort with us. These are all vulnerabilities that a computer, based in unyielding logic, is not subject to.

3.2 No Technical Expertise Needed

Because it is independent of the technical controls in the systems used, social engineering attacks can be carried out with minimal specialized knowledge on the part of the attacker. There is no need for experience in computer programming or thorough understanding of the underlying network structure in order to steal critical information through a conversation with an employee. All that is needed is enough of a backstory to seem plausible, a good sense of timing, a basic knowledge of the power names and common internal terminology, and anyone can don the mantle of social engineer.

This vulnerability that organizations have to social engineering attacks will continue to exist for the foreseeable future regardless of how advanced our technological systems become, as long as people are involved in some way. We see this over and over again in depictions of a technologically hyper-advanced future society as seen in science fiction movies and TV shows. How often does the protagonist (and sometimes the antagonist) use low-tech, social interaction-based methods to bypass security systems?

4. REASONS FOR RISE IN CYBERCRIME

It is difficult to obtain accurate numbers detailing the steady increase of cybercrime throughout the globe as the statistics are built on numbers of attacks, breaches, and other security events that are reported, leaving unreported numbers unaccounted for. However, CNN Money cites a report by Ponemon Institute that claims 47% of adults in the United States alone have had their personal information exposed, with 110 million of these data breaches occurring over a 12-month period from May 2013 to May 2014 as cited in (Pagliery, 2014). A world statistics portal reports that two of the most well-known companies suffering data breaches, Adobe and eBay, had 152 million and 145 million records stolen as of August 2015 (Statista, 2015). There are two major reasons for this rise in cybercrime over the last decade: the low risk and relative safety for attackers; and the increasing targets of opportunity provided by the Internet.

4.1 Low Risk

There is significant risk associated with an attempt to physically break into a house or business to steal money, equipment, or sensitive information. The likelihood of being caught in the act or leaving a plethora of DNA, fingerprints, shoeprints, hair and clothing particles, or security camera footage proving you were there is high. The effort and planning that are required to mitigate the risk of being caught or identified is correspondingly high. This level of preparation is not necessary for the criminal who uses a computer to attack the target's digital information and resources. Obscuring one's IP address and using other means to hide digital tracks is child's play for the amateur cracker. Specialized software to attack thousands of targets can be obtained for free through open-source means and run on Kali Linux, an operating system distribution specifically designed for network penetration (Kim, 2014). In comparison to a physical crime, the relative anonymity of the attacker is high and the time and resource requirements for the attack are minimal.

4.2 Increasing Targets of Opportunity

Every year, the world population continues its exponential growth. As more and more children are born, the number of potential computer users increases accordingly. Criminals largely tend to attack targets of opportunity. (Felson & Clarke, 1998) state:

"For the usual predatory crime to occur, a likely offender must find a suitable target in the absence of a capable guardian. This means that crime can increase without more offenders if there are more targets, or if offenders can get to targets with no guardians present. This also means that community life can change to produce more crime opportunities without any increase in criminal motivation" (Felson & Clarke, 1998).

Criminal acts, or attempts at criminal acts, involving the internet and digital connectivity will continue to increase as the target of opportunity increases. Internet connectivity has grown from 14.1% of the world's population in 2004 to 40.4% in 2014 (Internet Live Stats, 2014). Due to the increasing transition to digital records and transactions, as well as the sharing of personal information online, this target will continue to grow more and more enticing for those with the intent to blackmail, extort from, masquerade as, and steal from others.

5. IMPACT OF CYBERCRIME ON ORGANIZATIONS

Cybercrime is not an occurrence to be taken lightly. It may seem to be most devastating to the individual computer user due to the personal nature of the information compromised or funds stolen. However, organizations stand to lose much as well, and the damage done to them in the form of money, reputation, and time lost can be much more destructive in the long run due to the many people that are affected—employees and customers alike.

5.1 Financial Damage

The financial expense resulting from a successful network intrusion can be staggering. According to the (Ponemon Institute, 2015), in the United States, "The average cost for each lost or stolen record containing sensitive and confidential information increased from $201 to $217" and "the total average cost paid by organizations increased from $5.9 million to $6.5 million" from 2013 to 2014 (Ponemon Institute, 2015). The financial loss to an organization is not just calculated by how much money was taken by the attackers. It includes an estimate of the business that was lost due to non-availability of online resources in the case of a denial-of-service attack, as well as the cost of recovering deleted information in the event of a malicious attack involving the destruction of data. Additionally, the company may need to hire outside specialists to conduct a more thorough recovery, or pay for over-time for IT employees during the recovery operation.

5.2 Reputational Damage

A manager once worked for would frequently define trust as a "reservoir of fulfilled expectations". According to this definition, whatever an organization does that fulfills the expectations of its customers builds their trust and adds to the reservoir. Whenever those expectations are unfulfilled, that trust reservoir is diminished. A data breach, such as the one for Target in 2013, which resulted in over 40 million credit and debit card records compromised as well as names, addresses, and phone numbers of over 70 million customers (Yang & Jayakumar, 2014), is a huge drain on the trust of its customers. A loss of customer trust in a company leads to business lost for that company as they will be less likely to trust it with sensitive information required for business transactions. Additionally, when employees lose trust in their employer, they are more likely to start looking for work elsewhere. This is likely to negatively impact their dedication to the company and result in less productivity, creating a downward spiral for business. Loss of employee trust leads to higher attrition and emigration to competitors, continuing the downward trend for the organization that failed in its security.

5.3 Time Lost to Recovery

The third area of damage to an organization following a successful cyber-attack is time. Time drain results from having to recreate deleted records, notify employees and customers of the organization who have been victimized, and find and fix loopholes and harden the network to prevent further exploitation. (Grover et al., 2014) wrote that Sony Pictures Entertainment took over eight days to recover from the cyber-attack it suffered in December of 2014 (Grover et al., 2014), stating that the company "shut down its internal computer network…to prevent the data-wiping software from causing further damage, forcing employees to use paper and pen"(Grover et al., 2014). Network hardening and troubleshooting can be especially time-consuming for IT personnel and can take their focus off daily network operations, resulting in slower response time to help-desk requests and network maintenance. This creates a domino effect in which business efficiency falls even more due to the increased time it takes the rest of the organization to accomplish simple, daily operations requiring network resources.

6. RECOMMENDATIONS FOR PREVENTATIVE MEASURES AND SOLUTIONS TO VULNERABILITIES

Though the vulnerability of an organization to social engineering attacks will never be entirely removed, there are several preventative measures and solutions this vulnerability that can be taken. Because of the human element, simply implementing additional technical authorization mechanisms is not enough. Thorough training, frequent social engineering drills (such as bogus internal phishing attacks) and penetration tests, and an overall focus on organizational discipline are necessary.

6.1 Awareness Training

Enterprise Risk Management (Enterprise Risk Management, 2009) claims "training your employees is the best possible investment you could make to combat the threat of social engineering. An employee with an awareness of social engineering techniques will be able to proactively identify the traps and pitfalls commonly used" (Enterprise Risk Management, 2009). It further states:

Employee training and awareness programs should be tailored to meet audiences of varying technical levels. The "human firewall" can be strengthened by making employees fully aware of the organization's policies and procedures. Targeted and focused programs are the most effective long-term tool against social engineering. (Enterprise Risk Management, 2009)

6.2 Regular Training

An organization needs to conduct regular and redundant training on the means and methods of social engineering as well as the likelihood of attack. This training must be tightly ensured for each new employee before they gain access to the computer network or a put into any position that requires contact with non-employees. New employees are an easy target as they will likely not be as familiar with the faces that make up the organization as their experienced counterparts are.

6.3 Thorough Training

This awareness training needs to address as many aspects of social engineering as possible. It is impossible to perfectly predict that an intruder would use pretexting or phishing and not shoulder surfing or piggybacking. Even obscure means of attack should be discussed. A lack of breadth in what techniques are covered can result in employees being falsely confident that they can spot and defeat a social engineering attack, leaving them wide open to less commonly used methods.

6.4 Relevant Training

The training the organization conducts must be engaging, enjoyable, current, and relevant. It should not be so boring or ill-presented as to become a chore for the employees to have to sit through it. If the IT or management personnel are unable to come up with an enjoyable, engaging way to train the rest of the organization, outside subject matter experts should be brought in who specialize in conducting such training in an effective manner.

6.5 Frequent Social Engineering Drills and Penetration Tests

A way to bring home just how easy it is to become the victim of a social engineering attack is to conduct drills and unscheduled penetration tests on a regular basis. Many penetration testing companies provide this service as a part of their vulnerability assessment. Peter Kim describes an example of his penetration testing company conducting what he calls the "SMTP Attack":

In the following example, we are targeting the fake site bank.com, who has a subsidiary in Russia. The fake bank owns ru.bank.com and has MX records to that FQDN. Also, company.com (another fake company), owns us.company.com and has MX records for that FQDN. In this fake example, we purchase both the doppelganger domains uscompany.com and rucompany.com. If anyone mistypes an email to either domain, we will be able to inject ourselves into the middle of this conversation. By a few simple python scripts, when we receive an email from john@us.company.com to bob@rubank.com (mistyped doppelganger for ru.bank.com), our script will take that email and create a new email to bob@ru.bank.com (the proper email address) and sourced from john@uscompany.com (the mistyped doppelganger that we own). That means any reply response to John from Bob will come back through us. Now we have a full "Man in the MailBox" configured and can either just passively listen or attack the victims based on the trust factor they have for each other. (Kim, 2014)

However, the IT and facilities teams responsible for physical security should collaborate to conduct regular in-house drills, to reinforce the importance of vigilance on the employee population. Results of these drills and tests should be publicized (in an appropriate forum) for all to learn from and to showcase everyone's ongoing vulnerability.

6.6 Organizational Discipline

Organizations must create security policies that include specific, detailed steps to verifying the authenticity of a person interacting with the company. Additionally, policies and procedures must clearly and succinctly address all possible avenues of attack or areas where employee complacency creates gaping security holes. These policies should be published and posted in appropriately related areas such as at reception desks, by phones, and next to workstations, as well as in restrooms and breakrooms, and by watercoolers and coffee pots, where employees frequently go for downtime. Specific procedures should be simplified to a list for placement in areas where there is a high probability of attack, such as next to secretary telephones or at the reception desk.

Discipline must be a primary focus in the organization—policies must be taken seriously and followed. Management must enforce those policies and treat lapses in network security as seriously as they treat violations of physical security procedures. With the revolving door of employee turnover throughout the years, new employees who are uninformed and inexperienced will constantly join the organization. If there is an atmosphere of compliance with published policies and a commitment to safeguarding a secure environment, the risk that a new hire will remain ignorant or complacent toward security is significantly mitigated. Security issues should be a normal and common part of regular conversation in the workplace.

7. CONCLUSION

Social engineering will continue to threaten network security as long as we rely on people in the operation of organizations. As much as we may like to think that we can patch any tear, plug any hole, and close any loophole in the way that we protect ourselves and our data, this vulnerability cannot be completely removed. Every year, informed, experienced, and prepared employees leave a company for a variety of reasons and new hires take their place at the oar. These new employees lack the training and knowledge that their predecessors were given and will fall prey to old tricks, schemes, and cons that generations before them succumbed to unless they are intentionally prepared. The best we can do is to conduct regular, thorough, and relevant awareness training, frequent drills and realistic tests, and maintain a steady focus on the overall discipline of the organization. In this way, we will harden that component of the network that is the softest by nature—the human being.

REFERENCES

Braiker, H. B. (2004). *Who's pulling your strings?: How to break the cycle of manipulation and regain control of your life.* McGraw-Hill.

Curry, S. J. J. (2013). Instant-messaging security. In J. Vacca (Ed.), *Computer and information security handbook* (2nd ed., p. 727). Morgan Kaufmann. doi:10.1016/B978-0-12-803843-7.00051-X

Enterprise Risk Management. (2009, November). *Social engineering: People hacking.* Retrieved from https://www.emrisk.com/sites/default/files/newsletters/ERMNewsletter_november_2009.pdf

Felson, M., & Clarke, R. V. (1998). *Opportunity makes the thief: Practical theory for crime prevention* (Police Research Series Paper 98). Retrieved from https://webarchive.nationalarchives.gov.uk/20110218135832/rds.homeoffice.gov.uk/rds/prgpdfs/fprs98.pdf

Granger, S. (2010, November 3). *Social engineering fundamentals, part 1: Hacker tactics.* Retrieved from https://www.symantec.com/connect/articles/social-engineering-fundamentals-part-i-hacker-tactics

Grover, R., Hosenball, M., & Finkle, J. (2014, December 3). *Sony Pictures struggles to recover eight days after cyber attack.* Retrieved from https://www.reuters.com/article/2014/12/03/us-sony-cybersecurity-investigation-idUSKCN0JG27B20141203

Internet Live Stats. (2014, July 1). *Internet users in the world.* Retrieved from https://www.internetlivestats.com/internet-users/

Kim, P. (2014). *The hacker playbook: Practical guide to penetration testing.* Secure Planet.

Mitnick, K. D., & Simon, W. L. (2011). *Ghost in the wires: My adventures as the world's most wanted hacker.* Back Bay Books.

Pagliery, J. (2014, May 28). *Half of American adults hacked this year.* Retrieved from https://money.cnn.com/2014/05/28/technology/security/hack-data-breach/

Ponemon Institute. (2015, May). *2015 Cost of data breach study: United States.* Retrieved from IBM website: http://public.dhe.ibm.com/common/ssi/ecm/se/en/sew03055usen/SEW03055USEN.PDF

Simon, G. K. (2010). *In sheep's clothing: Understanding and dealing with manipulative people* (2nd ed.). Parkurst Brothers.

Statista. (2015, August). *Number of compromised data records in selected data breaches as of August 2015.* Retrieved from https://www.statista.com/statistics/290525/cyber-crime-biggest-online-data-breaches-worldwide/

Yang, J. L., & Jayakumar, A. (2014, January 10). *Target says up to 70 million more customers were hit by December data breach.* Retrieved from https://www.washingtonpost.com/business/economy/target-says-70-million-customers-were-hit-by-dec-data-breach-more-than-first-reported/2014/01/10/0ada1026-79fe-11e3-8963-b4b654bcc9b2_story.html

Chapter 4

Evaluating the Impact of Cybertheft Through Social Engineering and Network Intrusions

Nabie Y. Conteh
Southern University at New Orleans, USA

Anjelica B. Jackson
Southern University at New Orleans, USA

ABSTRACT

This chapter takes an in-depth look into the research literature to analyze and evaluate the role that social engineering plays in network intrusion and cybertheft. It will also discuss preventive measures and solutions to the threats and vulnerabilities that present themselves in the process of social engineering attacks. Social engineering is a means of stealing private data through tactics that make the victim feel comfortable to give their data. This kind of attack can cost individuals and organizations millions of dollars and block their access to data. The articles present multiple statistics that prove that the risk of social engineering attacks on individuals or organizations has increased tremendously. This new wave of communication has given hackers many opportunities to threaten security by tracking your email, phone, social networks, etc. Information detailing how users can be more aware of ways to protect their private information from attackers will also be presented.

DOI: 10.4018/978-1-7998-6504-9.ch004

INTRODUCTION

Over the years there have been many research studies conducted on social engineering, reporting on occurrences of attacks, tactics used to carry out attacks, how victims are affected, and ways to prevent future attacks. These studies have all had common results, which suggest that attackers are continuously successful due to the lack of preparation by the owners of the of the systems under attack. Users are urged to take a more active role in protecting themselves from attacks by staying abreast and knowledgeable of tactics, and prevention strategies. This paper will give users information provided by the research that will help them practice safe and effective data governance.

TOPIC ANALYSIS

In this paper social engineering is defined along with the types of social engineering attacks. In addition, this research will identify why cyber theft continues to advance at an alarming rate. Furthermore, psychological variables that contribute to vulnerabilities will be discussed. And finally, studies will be presented that identify key considerations regarding social engineering, testing and training, and point to how users can be coached to prevent attacks which offers a promising methodology to reduce system and user's risk.

Research indicates that "social engineering is a non-technical hack that uses trickery, persuasion, impersonation, emotional manipulation, and abuse of trust to gain information or computer system access through the human interface" (Thompson, 2006, p.222). Impersonation tactics are successful when the hacker can communicate the lingo of the victim company and policies. Manipulation tactics are performed by hackers who pretend to have lost company information, are unable to contact or get in touch with a source, and are unaware of common information that should not be forgotten. Hackers who are not using manipulation will contact the victim and ask for the information they are hoping to steal, which is known as a direct request approach (Thompson, 2006).

Types of Social Engineering Attacks

Below are some of the known social Engineering attacks:

- **Phishing:** Phishing scams attempt to obtain personal information such as names, addresses and other personal identifiable information (PII) such as social security numbers.

Phishing scams may embed links to redirect users to suspicious websites that appear legitimate. These types of scams create a sense of urgency to manipulate users to act in a manner that challenges good judgment.

- **Pretexting**: This type of social engineering attack is driven by a fabrication scenario attempting to confirm and steal personal information from a target. Advanced attacks attempt to exploit a weakness of an organization or company. This method requires the attacker to build a credible story that leaves little room to question doubt by a target. The strategy is to use fear and urgency while building a sense of trust with a victim to confirm or obtain sought information.
- **Baiting:** Baiting is similar to a phishing attack, but lures a victim through enticement strategies. Hackers use the lure of promised goods if a user surrenders log-in credentials to a specific site. Baiting schemes are not limited to, digital on-line schemes and can also be launched through the use of physical media.
- **Quid pro quo**: Similar to Baiting, but this type of threat is presented as a technical service in exchange for information. A common threat is for an attacker to impersonate an information technology representative and offer assistance to a victim who may be experiencing technical challenges. The attacker aims to launch malware on a user's system.
- **Tailgating:** This type of attack uses tailgating and piggybacking to gain access to restricted areas. This attack exposes those who have an ability to grant or gain access to a restricted area by an attacker who may impersonate delivery personnel or others who may require temporary access.

Preventive Measures Against Social Engineering

It is evident that regardless of how technologically secure a network seems the human element will always be a vulnerability. The success rate and the number of cybercrimes are steadily on the rise due to the level of anonymity social engineering offers malicious actors. Businesses have to remain cognizant of the various threat actors and their plethora of attacks so they are able to respond accordingly. There are technical and non-technical safeguards that can be implemented to lower the risk associated with social engineering to a tolerable level. Companies are adding multiple layers to their security schemes so that if the mechanism in the outer layer fails, a mechanism in at least one inner layer can help prevent a threat from turning into a disaster (Risk Mitigation). This concept is known as multi-layer defense or defense in depth. A good Defense in Depth structure includes a mixture of the following precautionary measures:

- **Security Policy**: A well written policy should include technical and nontechnical approaches that are downward driven by executive management. Every organization should integrate security into their operational objectives.
- **Education and Training:** Employees ought to be required to attend initial training during orientation and recurring refresher trainings. This builds awareness by exposing users to commonly employed tactics and behaviors targeted by a social engineer.
- **Network Guidance:** The organization have to safeguard the network by whitelisting authorized websites, using Network address translation (NAT), and disabling unused applications and ports. Network users have to maintain complex passwords that are changed every 60 days.
- **Audits and Compliance**: Organizations have to actively verify that their security policy is being adhered to. Some detective controls include reviewing network logs, re-validating employees' permissions, and checking desktop configurations at least bi-monthly.
- **Technical Procedures:** The network should have multiple layers of defence to protect data and core infrastructure. Software like Intrusion Prevention Systems (IPS), Intrusion Detection Systems (IDS) and firewalls should be installed on every device. Demilitarized Zones (DMZ), web filters and Virtual Private Network (VPN) should be installed on all external facing services.
- **Physical Guidance:** There is a range of options that can be implemented to protect physical assets. Using a combination of security guards, mantraps and security cameras to deter intruders from entering the premises is beneficial. In places where physical hardware is located businesses should employ multifactor authentication, biometrics or access control list before access is granted.

Research indicates that "social engineering is a kind of advanced persistent threat that gains private and sensitive information through social networks or other types of communication" (Nelson, Lin, Chen, Iglesias, & Li, 2016). The goal of this threat is for hackers to remain unnoticed to steal data from social networking accounts. Hackers seek out many targets, however, typical targets tend to be the Facebook accounts of government agencies, corporations, and school or high-profile users. Hackers are constantly becoming creative and looking for new practices to take advantage of the vulnerability of users. These threats to cybersecurity have rapidly increased in recent years (Nelson et al., 2016).

Reasons for Rise in Cybercrime

It is difficult to obtain accurate numbers detailing the steady increase of cybercrime throughout the globe as the statistics are built on numbers of attacks, breaches, and other security events that are reported, leaving unreported numbers unaccounted for. However, CNN Money cites a report by Ponemon Institute that claims 47% of adults in the United States alone have had their personal information exposed, with 110 million of these data breaches occurring over a 12-month period from May 2013 to May 2014 as cited in [11]. A world statistics portal reports that two of the most well-known companies suffering data breaches, Adobe and eBay, had 152 million and 145 million records stolen as of August 2015 [14]. There are two major reasons for this rise in cybercrime over the last decade: the low risk and relative safety for attackers; and the increasing targets of opportunity provided by the Internet. Social engineering's role in cyber theft and network intrusion is carried out through spear phishing. According to Trend Micro, "about 91% of targeted attacks using social engineering involve spear phishing emails or social network contacts" (Micro, 2012). Spear phishing is an email/contact that is sent to an organization as an attempt to steal data. These messages contain malicious content that is to be downloaded by the victim. Hackers frequently conduct this type of attack, because emailing and social networking are the most popular means of communicating for businesses (Nelson et al., 2016).

Financial Damage

The financial expense resulting from a successful network intrusion can be staggering. According to the [12], in the United States, "The average cost for each lost or stolen record containing sensitive and confidential information increased from $201 to $217" and "the total average cost paid by organizations increased from $5.9 million to $6.5 million" from 2013 to 2014 [12]. The financial loss to an organization is not just calculated by how much money was taken by the attackers. It includes an estimate of the business that was lost due to nonavailability of online resources in the case of a denial-of-service attack, as well as the cost of recovering deleted information in the event of a malicious attack involving the destruction of data. Additionally, the company may need to hire outside specialists to conduct a more thorough recovery, or pay for over-time for IT employees during the recovery operation.

Hackers have been working hard to increase the sophistication of their spear phishing attacks by using two methods. Their first method tricks the user into believing the threat came from a trusted person. The second method requires the hacker to make post for the public to see on social media that contain malicious files and links. For an attack to be successful, hackers do extensive research on organizations so their phony emails will be viewed as real. The more realistic an email or message is the better the outcome of the attack. (Nelson et al., 2016)

Hacking attacks are typically conducted by hackers who are seeking top secret information from the government, classified military data, and financial gain (Nelson et al., 2016). Research indicates that this attack is the root cause for yearly losses of millions of dollars. Ransomware is a form of social engineering that seeks financial gain from its victims. Once the malware infects your computer it will lock it and keep the owner from locating their files due to encryption. After the hacker perform the attack they will seek ransom from the victims (Savage, Coogan, & Lau, 2015). Researchers Savage, Coogan, and Lau (2015) stated that "over the past 12 months, 64 percent of ransomware attacks have been crypto ransomware, while 36 percent has been locker ransomware.

Not only has social engineering attacks such as spear phishing and ransomware been on the rise, other cybercrimes have increased as well. The reason for the expansion of cybercrime is the lack of skilled professionals available to tend to this matter. Research has indicated that "law enforcement often struggle to locate cybercrime offenders, because of factors such as access to a company's computer system can occur in many ways, by many different people, armed with an array of technical skills set" (Hewer, 2016). Because of this it is becoming easier for these cybercrime offenders to attack multiple times before they are caught by law enforcement. The article states that, "The world may only be one disruptive technology away from attackers gaining a runway advantage, meaning the internet would cease to be a trusted medium for communication or commerce" (Fraud and Risk, 2014).

Hewes's (2016) research indicates that "cybercrime is a criminal activity or a crime that involves the Internet, a computer system or computer technology." Some forms of cybercrime include phishing, identity theft, and infecting network and equipment. Research indicated that "In 2014, the U.S Department of Homeland Security estimated that it received nearly 100,000 cyber incident reports, and detected 64,000 vulnerabilities. It also states that, "they issued nearly 12,000 alerts or warnings, and responded to 115 major cyber incidents" (Hewes, 2016). These statistics show the alarming rate of how much cybercrime is being committed in the U.S.

Hewes's research indicated that "in 2016, 60% of small businesses were targeted by attackers". Many small and medium sized businesses found themselves defenseless as there was a surge increase in attack from 26% to 30%" (Hewes, 2016). In the year of 2014, large companies were not exempt from being targeted of attacks, which was a 40% increase since 2013" (Hewes, 2016). To put a halt to these cybercrime incidents, Congress has been taking charge by implementing new laws for 20+ years. (Hewes, 2016). The Computer Fraud and Abuse Act of 1984, is a law created to combat unauthorized access to devices and has been modified frequently since its inception due to cybercrime advancing and becoming more sophisticated" (Hewes, 2016).

Cybercrime offenders tend to be criminal groups, hackers/hacktivists, disgruntled insiders, bot-net operators, nations and agencies of nations, and terrorists. Individuals who commit fraud and extortion belong to criminal groups. Hackers/Hacktivists such as Anonymous, tend to hack systems to get their political message to the public. Individuals who are disgruntled contracts will consist of unexperienced employees who infect systems with malware, or they can be contractors who are hired to work for the organization. Members of terrorist groups job is to threaten national security by targeting critical infrastructures. Hackers known as bot-net operators facilitate phishing, and malware attacks to systems, and nations and agencies of nations job is to corrupt military operations and communication. (Hewes., 2016)

To defend against these groups, it is important for managers of companies to protect their cybersecurity from cybercrime offenders. Managers can benefit from paying close attention to some important factors such as, prevention, detection, legal compliance and timely notice to all stakeholders, equipment and network repair, and insurance liability coverage. When analyzing prevention methods, managers need to ask themselves questions such as: "has the organization developed a comprehensive cyber-security plan that addresses all the needs of the organization? Does it need to do so? Just how secure is the technology used by the organization?" (Hewes, 2016)

When a manager is analyzing detection, they need to be sure to have the best technology to defend against threats. Another important area of concern is that legal compliance and timely notice, is imperative to stay abreast of changes in law pertaining to regulations changing as crime advances. Backup systems need to be tested for functionality as precaution for an attack. Insurance liability coverage are necessary to possess in the event an organization is attacked and their data has been compromised, the policies can cover the acquired cost (Hewes, 2016).

There are many ways to reduce the risk of social engineering attacks such as awareness and vigilance. To protect your network from hackers it is important to download a firewall. To provide your computers and mobile devices with security, it is important to download a service such as McAfee LiveSafe service. When checking your email, pay close attention and never click on links and attachments from unknown parties. Whenever you are operating your social media accounts, post information that will not allow a hacker to steal your private information. (Nelson et al, 2016).

Another useful way to reduce the risk of social engineering is to report people who appear to be suspicious by asking for information they should not have such as: social security number and home address. It is important to remember that we have no control over the internet, therefore we should be wise and protect our personal information. When using websites that require important information, use the two-factor authentication methods, which identifies you by your password, and your possessions. Research states that "this a second layer of protection and should be enabled for sensitive information, such as banking information (Nelson et al., 2016).

Researcher Richardson and North (2017) indicate there are recommended ways for individuals and businesses to prevent ransomware infection. The first recommendation is to perform a backup on your device to restore data. The second recommendation is to never click on malicious email links and attachments. The third recommendation is patch and block to keep all your devices functioning and updated. The fourth recommendation is the drop and roll, which is turning off your device to eliminate more damage occurring after an attack. (Richardson & North, 2017).

The fifth recommendation is to make sure you are fully aware of the risk of malicious ransomware attacks. It is imperative that you create policies and procedures to defend your network from attacks. Always present the safes policies for users such as: password management, frequent security training, and procedure for employees dealing with finances or sensitive requests for fund transfers. Keep implementing periodic testing of employees to determine the effectiveness of their training, keep employees informed about the appropriate social media policy, and make sure employees keep the software on their personal devices updated (Richardson &North, 2017).

As stated in the article, "Incidents of Ransomware on the rise," 2016, The Federal Bureau of Investigation also recommends the following: keep employees knowledgeable of their particular roles in defending against ransomware, allow work to be performed by the lowest level of privilege to prevent the overuse of privileged accounts, facilitate appropriate network share permissions, directories, access controls, shut off macro scripts, and lastly implement restriction policies for software and operations to defend against ransomware infecting frequently used locations ("Incidents of Ransomware on the Rise," 2016).

CONCLUSION

Social engineering is an attack that plays on the innocent and naivety of victims. The trickery, manipulation, and impersonation are what entices the victim and causes them to let their guard down. Cyber criminals are attack victims in many ways at alarming rates in the U.S. Users need to make sure they are informed of the prevention/risk reduction policies presented in this paper. They need to familiarize themselves with the tactics of social engineers so they won't become a victim of an attack. They need to remember that attackers are seeking their private data such as banking information, social security number, address, etc.

Every year, informed, experienced, and prepared employees leave a company for a variety of reasons and new hires take their place at the oar. These new employees lack the training and knowledge that their predecessors were given and will fall prey to old tricks, schemes, and cons that generations before them succumbed to unless they are intentionally prepared. The best we can do is to conduct regular, thorough, and relevant awareness training, frequent drills and realistic tests, and maintain a steady focus on the overall discipline of the organization. In this way, we will harden that component of the network that is the softest by nature—the human being.

Remember, you receive spear phishing attacks daily in your email, so be sure to avoid attachments and links from unknown senders. If you follow these policies, you will greatly decrease your chances of being attacked. Although the threats of social engineering may not end anytime soon, users won't have to be defenseless against these threats, and will be able to fight the threats.

REFERENCES

Braiker, H. B. (2004). *Who's pulling your strings? How to break the cycle of manipulation and regain control of your life*. McGraw-Hill.

Fraud risk and cybercrime on the rise. (2014). *Money Marketing*, 29.

Hewes, J. A. (2016). Threat and Challenges of Cyber-Crime and the Response. *SAM Advanced Management Journal, 81*(2), 4-10.

Incidents of Ransomware on the rise. (2016, July 14). Retrieved from https://www.fbi.gov/news/stories/2016/april/incidents-of-ransomware-on-the-rise/incidents-ofransomware-on-the-rise

Micro, T. (2012). *Spear-Phishing Email: Most Favored APT Attack Bait*. Trend Micro. http://www.trendmicro.com.au/cloud-content/us/pdfs/security-intelligence/whitepapers/wp-spear-phishing-email-most-favored-apt-attackbait.pdf

Nelson, J., Lin, X., Chen, C., Iglesias, J., & Li, J. J. (2016). Social Engineering for Security Attacks. *ACM International Conference Proceeding Series, 1*. doi:10.1145/2955129.2955158

Pagliery, J. (2014, May 28). *Half of American adults hacked this year*. Retrieved from https://money.cnn.com/2014/05/28/technology/security/hack-data-breach/

Ponemon Institute. (2015, May). *2015 Cost of data breach study: United States*. Retrieved from IBM website: http://public.dhe.ibm.com/common/ssi/ecm/se/en/sew03055usen/SEW03055USEN.PDF

Richardson, R., & North, M. (2017). Ransomware: Evolution, Mitigation and Prevention. *International Management Review*, *13*(1), 10–21.

Savage, K., Coogan, P., & Lau, H. (2015). *The Evolution of Ransomware*. Academic Press.

State of Ransomware 2016: Understanding the Depth of the Ransomware Problem in the United States. (2016). Osterman Research, Inc.

Statista. (2015, August). *Number of compromised data records in selected data breaches as of August 2015*. Retrieved from https://www.statista.com/statistics/290525/cyber-crime-biggest-online-data-breachesworldwide/

Thompson, S. C. (2006). Helping the Hacker? Library Information, Security, and Social Engineering. *Information Technology and Libraries*, *25*(4), 222–225. doi:10.6017/ital.v25i4.3355

Vulnerabilities, C. (2017). Article. *Credit Union Magazine*, *83*(1), 15.

Zetter, K. (2015, September 17). *Hacker lexicon: A guide to Ransomware, the scary hack that's on the rise*. Retrieved from Security: https://www.wired.com/2015/09/hacker-lexicon-guideransomware-scary-hack-thats-rise/Zetter

Chapter 5
Industry Trends in Computer Software

Sara A. Syed
University of Maryland Global Campus, USA

ABSTRACT

In the modern age of technological innovation, organizations are evolving rapidly due to the abundance of opportunities. This evolution has provided organizations with the ability to leverage technology for their benefit; however, cybersecurity risks have also developed due to the emerging trends. As the software industry faces a surge of emerging trends, it is critical to address the impeding threats to our cybersecurity infrastructure. The computer software industry is classified under the North American Industry Classification System (NAICS) code 511210 for software publishers. The software development market has experienced an exponential growth as a shift to the cloud has rendered a greater need for cutting edge technology, and this trend is projected to continue.

INTRODUCTION

In the modern age of technological innovation, organizations are evolving rapidly due to the abundance of opportunities. This evolution has provided organizations with the ability to leverage technology for their benefit, however, cybersecurity risks have also developed due to the emerging trends. As the software industry faces a surge of emerging trends, it is critical to address the impeding threats to our cybersecurity infrastructure. This paper intends to analyze the leading industry trends in software services and will highlight the findings of the top three trends

DOI: 10.4018/978-1-7998-6504-9.ch005

developing in the software industry and their significance to the overall development of the cybersecurity field.

FINDINGS

The computer software industry is classified under the North American Industry Classification System (NAICS) code 511210 for Software Publishers. The software development market has experienced an exponential growth as a shift to the cloud has rendered a greater need for cutting edge technology and this trend is projected to continue. According to the MarketLine Industry Profile, "In 2024, the United States software market is forecast to have a value of $306.6 billion, an increase of 53% since 2019" (Hoovers, 2020b). The need for automation, reduction of time-to-market, cost reduction, adherence to laws and regulations, and a guaranteed return of investment are leading factors propelling the industry's growth (Hoovers, 2020b). The recent market findings suggest Open Source Software (OSS), Artificial Intelligence (AI), Software as a Service (SaaS) and as the latest trends for growth in the software industry.

TOP TRENDS OF THE SOFTWARE INDUSTRY

Open Source Software (OSS)

In recent years, Open Source Software has emerged as a revolutionary alternative to traditional proprietary methods. Dong et al (2018) describes open software development as "The online workforce contributes (sic) to the code base of OSS, making it essentially a result of crowdsourcing of the software innovation projects." In comparison to higher costs of licensing proprietary software and the rigidity of customization, OSS provides a cost-effective collaboration of source code available for public use, allowing the end user to make modifications to suit their program needs. OSS has gained traction in the industry which can be attributed to the notion that "many eyes" communities of developers collaborating on OSS leads to programs that have fewer vulnerabilities leading to fewer security concerns (Synopsis, 2018). The appeal of OSS for businesses can be accounted to the collective nature since they can innovate much faster because "they don't need to reinvent core functionality" (Synopsys, 2020). Organizations can readily adapt to market changes as software testing and deployment are supported by multiple contributors. An open source audit of 17 industries found that open source components were detected in every software application of those industries. Approximately 64% of codebase in Artificial

Intelligence had open source elements, while 68% of open source code was discovered in Software as a Service (Synopsys, 2020). The data collected is an insurmountable indication of how the industry is shifting from the conventional closed source business model to the more viable OSS model. OSS movement is undeniably one of the major trends that is set to dominate the commercial software market.

Artificial Intelligence (AI)

Artificial Intelligence technology varies from previous cohorts of IT in its ability to learn and update using computational data (Huang et al, 2019). For a machine to be considered intelligent, it must process massive amounts of complex algorithms fast and make precise predictions. Ever since the inception of Artificial Intelligence there has been an upsurge of AI-based applications slowly integrating into our daily lives. Early applications of AI include autonomous cars, digital voice assistants, facial recognition, and smart hubs; and with each new iteration it brings the software industry closer to the future that is Artificial Intelligence. AI is often dubbed as the next force of digital disruption as it becomes more mainstream in day to day business operations. For businesses to stay relevant, they must adopt AI functionality to improve their Information Technology infrastructure. Research conducted by Artificial Intelligence Software: Market Report (2019) indicates that "25% of all job-based tasks will be automated by 2019. Many experts suggest that by 2050, machines will reach the level of human intelligence." The AI market promises huge potential across various industry sectors as the implementation of AI-based technology can deliver value to end users while reducing costs and improving productivity for businesses. Acquisdata (2020a) forecasts that "AI can improve productivity by more than 40% at organizations." The market for AI is inevitably growing and this transformation can be seen across industry sectors such as retail, transportation, manufacturing, and banking as AI-based applications are trending.

Software as a Service (SaaS)

With the development of the internet, technology has evolved at a global scale uprooting the primitive constraints of traditionally bound hardware to a virtual environment, allowing businesses to gain a competitive advantage. Virtualization of the software industry has gained drastic momentum as companies are shifting towards the adoption of cloud application services such as Software as a Service (SaaS) to support their clients. SaaS supports a delivery model where the software is hosted off-site by a third party, delivered via the web and customers pay a subscription fee, in place of a license. Organizations can mitigate the capital cost of implementing SaaS solutions since the architecture is supported by the service provider, combined with benefit of not having to maintain a large overhead of technical staff to operate the application. The SaaS provider is liable for delivering, securing, and managing the application, data and all essential infrastructure (Raghavan, K.R., Nargundkar, 2020). To sustain the workload, organizations may stipulate the conditions for elasticity to adapt to the needs of the workload to manage costs on the run as demands dictate. Guidelines from Cloud Security Alliance (2017) state that "Rapid elasticity allows consumers to expand or contract the resources they use from the pool (provisioning and deprovisioning), often completely automatically". This scalability is a key reason for the growth and development of SaaS since businesses can manage resources such as server utilization as their demands grow or decrease. Indubitably SaaS is predicted to be the "largest market segment, which is forecast to grow to $116 billion next year due to the scalability of subscription-based software" (Gartner, 2019). With the promises of low costs, swift deployment, and vast opportunities for a Return on Investment (ROI), it is certain that SaaS is a rising trend that is not showing signs of slowing down.

AN IMPORTANT EMERGING ISSUE

The unfolding COVID-19 pandemic has led to proliferated risks of cyber threats to SaaS applications. Data derived from Acquisdata (2020b) states that "Business will fall victim to a ransomware attack every 14 seconds by 2019 and every 11 seconds by 2021". In 2017, one of the largest credit bureaus, Equifax had a data breach due to vulnerabilities found in the software. The infraction exposed 147 million customers, costing the company $425 million in settlement, making it one of largest cybercrimes to date (Swinhoe, 2020). Most recently, IT services giant, Cognizant became compromised by ransomware affecting its internal systems and thrusting the company into crisis management and costing the company millions in damages. These incidents highlight the dangers of providing proprietary information to third party custodians of data and trusting that these vendors will be responsible with the safety and security of data.

Emerging risks in cybersecurity include several items that create concerns for organizations such as loss of control, limited customization, slower speed, and security risks (CompTIA, 2020). In a SaaS agreement, the organization leverages the vendor due to the affordability and flexibility offered, but this poses the issue of losing control on the data and accepting risks from the vendor. Traditionally, SaaS providers have predefined templates of the software which limits the scope for future change unless the software developer is willing to modify the application. If the vendor does not have proper load balancers in place or fail over servers, service could be disrupted easily. A Distributed Denial of Service (DDOS) attack can then easily destabilize a SaaS provider if mitigation tools, techniques and procedures are not in place. This can severely harm the reputation and image of the organization which can impact sales and future growth. As issues emerge from the vulnerabilities in trending software, organizations are modifying their approach to attest to data control and security procedures native to cybersecurity.

CONCLUSION

While competition and globalization has compelled organizations to adopt technology to leverage their growth, there are collateral risks that also are on the rise. Cybercrime is becoming more prevalent due to the nature of the technology. In fact, according to the World Economic Forum, "Cyberthreats have become one of the top ten global risks today, and among the most likely high-impact risks" (Acquisdata, 2020b). Although there are emerging issues, with every known issue there are opportunities an organization may pursue, such as industry guidelines to exercise the cybersecurity initiatives for countering software threats and vulnerabilities. This may include following guidelines issued under the National Institute of Standards and Technologies (NIST) or the International Organization for Standardizations (ISO). Adopting these guidelines will help companies manage risk as they add services and products to their business portfolio to remain competitive.

REFERENCES

Acquisdata Industry Profile: Artificial Intelligence Software Industry. (2020a). Acquisdata Global Industry SnapShot. *Artificial Intelligence Software Industry*, *295*, 1–48.

Acquisdata Industry Profile. (2020b). *Cybersecurity Industry*. Acquisdata Global Industry SnapShot Cybersecurity Industry.

Artificial Intelligence Software. Market Report. (2019). In *Artificial Intelligence Software*. Acquisdata, Inc. https://bi-gale-com.ezproxy.umgc.edu/global/article/GALE%7CA601435798?u=umd_umuc&sid=ebsco

Cloud Security Alliance. (2017). *Cloud Security Alliance's Security Guidance for Critical Areas of Focus in Cloud Computing*. https://cloudsecurityalliance.org/artifacts/security-guidance-v4/

CompTIA. (2020). *What Is SaaS*. https://www.comptia.org/content/articles/what-is-saas

Dong, J. Q., Wu, W., & Zhang, Y. (2018). The faster the better? Innovation speed and user interest in open source software. *Information & Management.* https://doi-org.ezproxy.umgc.edu/10.1016/j.im.2018.11.002

Gartner. (2019, November 13). *Gartner Forecasts Worldwide Public Cloud Revenue to Grow 17% in 2020* [Press release]. https://www.gartner.com/en/newsroom/press-releases/2019-11-13-gartner-forecasts-worldwide-public-cloud-revenue-to-grow-17-percent-in-2020#:~:text=Software%20as%20a%20service%20(SaaS,software%20(see%20Table%201).&text=IaaS%20is%20forecast%20to%20grow,rate%20across%20all%20market%20segments.

Hoovers. (2020a). Industry Custom Report: IT Services in the United States. *Hoovers Research Database.* https://app-avention-com.ezproxy.umgc.edu/API/Report/ApplinkPDF/API/Custom/GetIndustryReport.aspx?Report=MARKET RESEARCH&Type=GetReport&FileFormat=PDF&ReportID=60432&FileNa me=0072-2313-2019.pdf&VendorName=Datamonitor

Hoovers. (2020b). Industry Custom Report: Software in the United States. *Hoovers Research Database.* https://app-avention-com.ezproxy.umgc.edu/API/Report/ApplinkPDF/API/Custom/GetIndustryReport.aspx?Report=MARKET RESEARCH&Type=GetReport&FileFormat=PDF&ReportID=60316&FileNa me=0072-0381-2019.pdf&VendorName=Datamonitor

Huang, M.-H., Rust, R., & Maksimovic, V. (2019). The Feeling Economy: Managing in the Next Generation of Artificial Intelligence (AI). *California Management Review, 61*(4), 43–65. doi:10.1177/0008125619863436

Srinivasa Raghavan, R., Jayasimha, K. R., & Rajendra, V. N. (2020). Impact of software as a service (SaaS) on software acquisition process. *Journal of Business & Industrial Marketing, 35*(4), 757–770. https://doi-org.ezproxy.umgc.edu/10.1108/JBIM-12-2018-0382

Swinhoe, D. (2020, April 17). *The 15 biggest data breaches of the 21st century.* CSO Online. https://www.csoonline.com/article/2130877/the-biggest-data-breaches-of-the-21st-century.html

Synopsis: Open Source Security and Risk Analysis. (2018). *Network Security, 3*(6). https://doi-org.ezproxy.umgc.edu/10.1016/S1353-4858(18)30051-5

Synopsys. (2020). Synopsys 2020 Open Source Security and Risk Analysis Report. *Synopsys.* https://www.synopsys.com/content/dam/synopsys/sig-assets/reports/2020-ossra-report.pdf

Chapter 6

The Analysis of Top Cyber Investigation Trends

Alicia Leslie-Jones
iD https://orcid.org/0000-0003-1539-1975
University of Maryland Global Campus, USA

ABSTRACT

Cybersecurity is an ever-evolving area of technology. As such, there will always be myriad trends to consider. Through the progression of cybersecurity comes the increased need for organizations to keep pace with the rapid development of technology. However, the current skills gap of cybersecurity professionals has overwhelmingly become a cause for concern. The spread of cloud computing has created a need for new cloud forensics procedures, and the use of internet-connected medical devices has added concerns for the information security structure of many organizations. In order to resolve these issues, proper vulnerability testing and implementation of new processes to keep up with the changes in technology have to be introduced to reduce the possibility of hacking incidents and aid in remediation. If more organizations leverage the skills and personnel available to them, there are ways to reduce the skills gap and other issues affecting cybersecurity.

INTRODUCTION

As the world continues to increase its dependency on technology and its associated devices, so will the need for cybersecurity. This rise is a direct reflection of cybercrimes that have been committed and those anticipated for the future. Demands for digital forensics and cybersecurity and investigation professionals will not cease. Unfortunately, the lack of personnel qualified to meet the need of this industry will

DOI: 10.4018/978-1-7998-6504-9.ch006

remain an issue due to a skills gap (Griffin, 2020). It is estimated that it will take as long as 20 years to close this gap. As advancements in cloud technology and computing have been made, the need for forensic analysis procedures in cloud-based environments has increased. This is due mostly to its volatility (Baldwin, et al. 2018, pp. 324–325). Additionally, the constant rise in malware and ransomware attacks on medical centers and other healthcare-related organizations puts the expanded use of internet-connected medical devices at an increased risk for hacking events (Matthews, 2020). From these trends, several issues begin to emerge. A greater need for techniques to properly secure internet-connected devices and the preservation of forensic investigative findings in cloud environments arises. This further develops into concerns about the legal qualifications, certification, and investigative methodology of the cyber-forensic investigator or analyst. This chapter will provide an in-depth look at these emerging issues and ways to combat their effect on cybersecurity professions, related devices, and the performance of legally admissible cyber investigations.

BACKGROUND

In an occupational field that continuously undergoes technological transformations such as cyber investigations, an exact match for this labor industry does not exist. However, the North American Industry Classification System (NAICS) code 541513 for computer facilities management services is a close match for the duties and responsibilities of a professional in the field of cyber investigations. Industry codes 922110 and 56161 cover the investigative and law enforcement aspect of this industry by including sheriff's offices that conduct court functions and investigative services (NAICS Code, 2020). Additionally, the Standard Occupational Classification (SOC) code that defines information security analysts (15-1212) who monitor and provide protection for computer networks through the implementation of security controls and generates mitigation procedures aids in the definition of the task requirements help to outline this labor industry. Digital forensics analysts could be classified by 33-3021, which covers investigators who assist in the prevention or solution of crimes. Lastly, computer systems administrators (15-1244) who perform system backups and review the operating system and associated applications logs also reflect the duties of those who fulfill cyber-investigations and digital forensics roles (2018 SOC System, 2020).

With a multitude of occupational descriptions and categories, cybersecurity covers a broad spectrum of duties and responsibilities. Becoming a professional with a high level of expertise in this field requires a never-ending quest for knowledge and the ability to adapt as this field continues to change. Unlike many other fields, cybersecurity is primarily considered to be a reactive career field. Quite often, the high degree of cyber-crime methodology tends to advance quicker than processes for protecting against them. In many ways, cybersecurity can feel like fighting a battle from the losing side. It is the mission of the cybersecurity professional to use acquired technical knowledge and expertise to suggest and implement the best business practices for protecting their entities or organizations.

COMBATING CYBERSECURITY AND INVESTIGATION SHORTFALLS

This chapter will outline three of the top trending cybersecurity and investigation issues and the ways in which these issues should be further investigated and remediated to prevent further shortfalls. If these issues remain unresolved and unmitigated, cybersecurity will become less of a preventative measure for many organizations and explicitly become a reactionary force. As hacking becomes more prevalent in all areas of the technology-filled lifestyle to which this world has grown accustomed, more must be done to lessen its effect on people, businesses, and other entities. As helpful as technology has become, it also has the ability to bring about the demise of those organizations that do not do their part to effectively safeguard against cyberattacks and secure the data stored within their systems. The proper handling of cybersecurity cannot solely be done through the use of technology-based tools. The use of human interaction will always be necessary for the monitoring, testing and the implementation of cybersecurity best practices.

Through comprehensive research of top trends of cybersecurity and, more specifically, within the area of cyber-investigations, several issues of importance have emerged. The first issue presented is not having enough qualified cybersecurity professionals to fill the millions of reported occupational vacancies. Additionally, an issue with the preservation of investigative findings in cloud computing environments while ensuring the certifications and legal qualifications of the cyber-investigator or digital forensics analyst arises. Lastly, there is a serious need for the hardening of software on internet-connected medical devices and networks upon which they reside. These issues will continue to evolve as technological advancements to information technology (IT), information assurance (IA), and cybersecurity continue to be made, and highly-skilled hackers attempt to circumvent their associated security postures.

ISSUES, CONTROVERSIES, PROBLEMS

Of the top trends that were researched, the growing skills gap of cybersecurity professionals seems to be the most prevalent. With an 11% increase of cybercrimes, hacking, and the use of malware across all industries, organizations are demanding experienced cybersecurity professionals (Jones, 2020). Unfortunately, the demands for sufficient experience and expertise currently cannot be met. According to DDLS Australia (2019), it is projected that there will be approximately 3.5 million cybersecurity employment opportunities that will remain unfilled through 2021. Jones (2020), finds that almost 40% of global directors are grappling with the demand for cybersecurity professionals as cybersecurity professionals are struggling to keep pace with the speed of technological changes. As a result, the lack of qualified professionals has created an over dependency on technological resources to fulfill the duties of proficient personnel. Most establishments need more cybersecurity professionals for their organizations than they have available to properly maintain and effectively respond to cybersecurity incidents and data breaches. Currently, nearly 70% of organizational decision-makers have concluded that cybersecurity roles are extremely difficult to fill. Additionally, over 80% feel that this presents medium to high-level risks to the cybersecurity posture and remediation responses of their organizations (Jones, 2020).

According to Cobb (2018), a major issue affecting the cybersecurity skills gap is the lack of gender diversity which contributes to the shortfall of qualified professionals. Women make up over 40% of undergraduate information technology and security degree holders. In addition, they hold 50% of master's degrees or higher in the cybersecurity profession compared to 45% of their male counterparts. Yet somehow, they continue to be under-represented in this career field. This is due in part to the ongoing gender wage gap and the lack of opportunities provided to women. These practices, both biased and unbiased, are negatively affecting the ability to close the cyber-skills gap. Studies have shown that the employment of diverse teams of cybersecurity professionals are more proficient in problem solving and critical thinking (Cobb, 2018). The inclusion of more women in cybersecurity roles can positively contribute to the wide range of skills, perspectives, and expertise of any team.

Cloud computing has emerged as a rapidly growing technological field which leads to an additional need for cybersecurity and creates a necessity for the transition in digital forensics techniques to cloud computing forensics. According to the National Institute of Standards and Technology (NIST) Internal Report 8006, "Cloud computing forensic science is the application of scientific principles, technological practices, and derived and proven methods to reconstruct past cloud computing events through the identification, acquisition, preservation, examination, interpretation, and reporting of potential digital evidence" (pp. 2). With the rapid development of cloud technology, the way in which data is stored and recovered is continuing to change (Baldwin, et al. 2018, p. 311). Cloud computing environments have an increased volatility of data and for that reason they are considered some of the most valuable entities for those who launch cyberattacks (Baldwin, et al. 2018, p. 325). This volatility of data is a direct correlation to the cloud computing environment's use of virtual machines (VM) that allow for all data to be erased when it is shut down or restarted. For this reason, cloud forensics is currently treated as a subset of network forensics (Alex & Kishore, 2017). Increased cloud computing has the ability to increase the likelihood of malware and ransomware attacks on a larger scale due to the shared nature of cloud computing architecture.

The level of service provided by different cloud providers such as software as a service (SaaS), platform as a service (PaaS) and infrastructure as a service (IaaS) have different security requirements for the provider and host which can have an effect on how cybersecurity and cyber-investigations are handled by each provider and hosted organization (Baldwin, et al. 2018, p. 312). SaaS providers manage all aspects of the cloud experience from the network and storage to the data and applications used in the cloud environment. PaaS providers manages an organization's cloud environment with the exception of any data or applications. IaaS providers are sometimes considered "bare-bones" as they only provide the infrastructure or hardware for the cloud, all operating systems and associated middleware, data and applications are implemented by the hosted organization.

In addition to a difference in service models, the cloud environment also differs in deployment models and characteristics. Cloud computing can be deployed as public, private, hybrid, or community cloud environments. In a public cloud deployment, a company provides services and resources to multiple organizations for free or pay-per-use. Examples of companies that provide this type of deployment model are Microsoft's Azure, Amazon's AWS, and Google's Compute. Private cloud deployments are overall the same as public cloud except for the fact that it is only used by one organization and has authorized users for the internalized cloud environment. This form of cloud deployment is often used by corporate entities. Community cloud environments are similar to the private cloud, aside from the fact that a group of organizations instead of a single organization has access to the resources and infrastructure. Common users of community cloud environments are government organizations and banks. Hybrid environments are simply a mix of the cloud deployments detailed above.

During its inception, digital forensics heavily relied on the ability to physically access and perform investigative analysis of a computing device. This presents an issue for the proper acquisition of data for processing and investigative analysis. The state of the data, whether it be at rest, in motion or in execution, can further complicate data acquisition. This is because the different states of the data can modify where the data is physically located on the network at the time of investigation. As cloud computing has and will continue to grow, physically inaccessible devices as well as shared infrastructure will continue to be an issue for conducting proper cyber-investigations and analysis procedures (Alex & Kishore, 2017). The sharing of infrastructure or multi-tenancy and the service level used by the hosted organization presents investigators with additional challenges such as the issue of decreased control of the environment and devices being investigated. In addition, the location of the data centers can change the jurisdiction of the investigation. Cloud service providers have data centers worldwide, so the use of cross-border law is relevant to investigations in the cloud environment.

Due to the level of access to the cloud environment, a digital forensics investigator may need the assistance from a third party like the cloud service providers to perform data collection functions. The personnel assigned to assist with the collection of data may not have the certifications necessary to ensure the integrity of the data collection procedures for use in a judicial environment (Alex & Kishore, 2017). In the cloud environment the outcomes of the investigation are largely dependent on the involvement and truthfulness of the cloud service providers. As the cloud service provider collects data, it has the ability to tamper with it prior to access being given to a digital forensics investigator. This causes issues for the chain of custody, validity of the reported findings, and legality of the data collected. The chain of custody is significant to any cyber-investigation, as it gives the chronological details of when and how the information is collected, the analysis procedures and its organization for presentation in court (Alex & Kishore, 2017). Another issue presented through the use of a cloud computing environment is that it makes it impossible for the digital crime scene to be reconstructed for explanation in a courtroom. This also removes the attribute of repeatability and reproducibility for the quality assurance of the investigative results to be replicated by another forensic analyst.

To combat this, several new cloud-based tools have been introduced in response to the move to cloud computing forensic needs. Forensic OpenStack Tools, or FROST, is a cloud-based option that provides forensics tools for the OpenStack that has been built into any IaaS cloud platform (Baldwin et al., 2018). This tool provides a reliable and trusted way to perform the acquisition of virtual disks, guest firewall logs, and API logs. Functionality of this tool resides at the cloud management level instead of the virtual machine (Dykstra & Sherman, 2013). Also, there is a cloud-based tool called OWADE that allows for the reconstruction of online credentials and web browsing history. Lastly, Amazon has introduced CloudTrail in their Amazon Web Services (AWS) environment to provide logging capabilities. However, these tools do not have the same level of capabilities as the industry standard tools. Forensic tools such as Forensic Tool Kit (FTK), EnCase, Snort, Wireshark, Sleuthkit, and

X-Ways are a few of the industry standard tools. FTK has the ability to perform memory and drive imaging remotely. The e-discovery suite within EnCase can perform the acquisition of drive images and offline examinations (Baldwin et al., 2018) Snort and Wireshark provide network traffic capture, packet logging and analysis resources. Sleuthkit performs data recovery and the analysis of forensic images. With the increase in cloud computing these tools are quickly becoming insufficient for conducting proper cloud computing forensic investigation procedures.

Another trend on the rise in cybersecurity is the use of internet connected medical devices (Matthews, 2020). The use of an internet of things (IoT) fitness device such as a Fitbit or an Apple Watch have gained traction in the preceding years and it is presumed that internet connected medical devices will follow that trend. These devices give medical professionals the ability to remote access them, which is helpful and convenient for quick changes to medication dosing and reviews of how the implanted devices are working for the patient. However, it also poses a possibly fatal hacking risk to the patients in which they are implanted. With the increased prevalence of cloud computing, the use of internet connected devices have an enhanced risk of being hacked.

Healthcare organizations need to take a more proactive approach to their cybersecurity. Laxed security practices such as unsecured network connections, faulty coding, and the lack of security embedded into the initial design of devices can make them prone to cyberattacks. Although it is more likely that common IoT devices such home automation appliances, medical record programs, and storage systems to be attacked, it does not completely take away the possibility of internet connected medical devices being targeted by malicious hackers (Jaret, 2018). Implantable pacemakers, insulin pumps, and drug infusion pumps with internet connectivity from a variety of manufacturers have been found to possess vulnerabilities that can be exploited (Jaret, 2018). As previously mentioned, much of organizational computing is moving to cloud environments. This not only puts the internet connected medical devices at risk, but the networks to which they are connected as well.

Internet connected medical devices can be viewed as a network endpoint or as a small computer connected to hospital, manufacturer or cloud based organizational hosted servers. As such these devices are susceptible to hacking not only of the device, but the associated network (Li et al., 2018, pp. 16–17). Healthcare organizations need to prioritize the potential risk of medical device hacking and identify ways to mitigate it. These risks are commonly mitigated through the use of three techniques: the use of firewalls, an intrusion detection system, and the use of a device management system. Firewalls are considered a traditional way to prevent attacks, but this method is only useful if the intrusion is detected prior to access to the organization's internal network. The use of an intrusion detection system is only as good the habits of the networks users as this technique has the ability to provide administrators with false-positive reporting. Although a device management system can be useful, their ability to protect the network depends on how quickly these systems can identify an infected device out possibly thousands of connected devices before the attack is initiated (Li et al., 2018). Hackers can infiltrate these connected medical devices by simply cracking the passwords with a variety of methods and tools. Hackers also have the option to purchase a new device and gain root access using the manufacturers default credentials. Once they have gained root access, they can use various hacking techniques to connect it to the healthcare organization's network. Once the hacker obtains access, they will be able to intercept the inbound and outbound network traffic, often without detection for extended periods of time causing massive compromises to the organization's data.

MORE ISSUES, CONTROVERSIES, AND PROBLEMS

With cybersecurity and its continuous evolution, the ethics of those who conduct cyber-investigations plays a factor. Unlike the occupational fields of medicine and law, cybersecurity and more specifically digital forensics does not have an all-encompassing code of ethics. Without a code of ethics, cyber-investigators will encounter situations for which no guidance exists, and in those types, determinations will often be made by free will, internalized ideas of legality and organizational environments. Without a defined certification requirements and standardization of processes, digital forensics and cyber-investigations risk being considered "junk science" (Seigfried-Spellar et al., 2017). However, others believe that with the growth of subsets of cyber-investigations such as cloud forensics that there is not enough knowledge of the associated technologies to develop such a code. Regardless, there needs to be guidance for professional behavior that is not left solely up to the individual or the organization by which they are employed at any particular time. If this continues to be the case, there will be no consequences for those who use questionable methods to conduct investigations. Without an overarching code of ethics, individuals who conduct digital forensics investigations can move on to different organizations with different requirements and continue to fulfill the same type of roles without accountability for past behaviors. This would make problematic practices the rule rather than the exception.

In addition to issues with the absence of a code of ethics for digital forensics, there is also no clearly defined credentialing path. Someone can choose either vendor-neutral or vendor-specific certifications. The only determining factor for which certifications to pursue are directly related to personal thoughts or ideas and those listed in the requirements of job postings. Common vendor-neutral certifications include the Certified Forensic Computer Examiner (CFCE) from the International

Association of Computer Investigative Specialists (IACIS), and the Certified Computer Examiner (CCE) certification from the International Society of Forensic Computer Examiners (ISFCE). Probably the most well-known and widely accepted certifications are the Global Information Assurance Certifications (GIAC). These certifications are widely trusted by government organizations such as the U.S. National Security Agency (NSA). Some of GIAC's certifications include: GIAC Certified Forensic Analyst (GCFA), GIAC Advanced Smartphone Forensics (GASF), GIAC Certified Forensic Examiner (GCFE), GIAC Network Forensic Analyst (GNFA), and GIAC Reverse Engineering Malware (GREM). The most common vendor specific certifications are the EnCase Certified Engineer (EnCE) and AccessData Certified Examiner (ACE). These two certifications test proficiency with specific tools like FTK technology and increases professional credibility for testifying about digital forensic data and processes in a court of law. Each of these exams vary in testing procedures, training requirements, certification renewal and expiration policies. With all of these certifications available, and prerequisite exam training prices as high as $2,800 for becoming a qualified digital forensic investigator or analyst is not only confusing, it is also very expensive.

One of the top threats to cybersecurity and preventative measures for cybersecurity is personnel. A level of accountability must apply to more than just the cyber-professionals and digital investigators. Personnel at all levels of the organization are to be held responsible for the security of their systems. Too often organizations focus on the responsibility of the IT and cyber-professionals in the organization to secure the systems and not enough emphasis on the cyber-awareness and security practices of the entire workforce. Most successful hacking incidents are due to bad or laxed information security practices. Additionally, organizations tend to only focus on the external threat when the internal threats are just as if not more likely to be the source of a data breach. Insider threats have the ability to bypass most safeguards and intrusion detection because the individual is an authorized user of the system. Allowing personnel to have more access to the systems than necessary to complete the duties and responsibilities of their role in the organization rather than a policy of least privilege is an enabling environment for insider threats.

SOLUTIONS AND RECOMMENDATIONS

As it pertains to the skills gap of cybersecurity personnel, a viable option for many organizations is to increase the skill level by cross-training and investing in the personnel that are already employed by the entity. This has the ability to offset the current shortage of skills (Griffin, 2020). In a DDLS survey, it was reported that ensuring that the skills of the team kept up with the constant changes in cybersecurity was seen as one of the major challenges. This is often due to the fact that organizations do not invest in the talent that already exists within (DDLS Australia, 2019, p. 8). By ignoring their talent, the company promotes an organizational environment with a high turnover rate due to personnel feeling undervalued. On the other end of the spectrum, some organizations assign too many additional duties to employees that already feel overworked or they are given additional roles to fill without proper compensation. Many organizations do not properly promote from within and this leads to an environment of mistrust and quite often, employees will leave their place of employment due managerial shortcoming and lack of inclusivity. Organizations need to be mindful of the environment and corporate culture they create.

With the shortage of trained professionals, organizations should move from the idea of employing the person who meets every qualification, to personnel that best fits the requirements and are considered trainable in areas that they may lack expertise. It is not logical to expect expertise without job openings that will allow personnel to gain experience. Also, experience, educational and compensation for the roles should make sense. Too often there are job postings for entry level jobs that require five or more years of experience and a minimum education requirement of a master's degree with minimum wage compensation. It is understood that the cost of living varies based on the location of employment, but compensation should be reasonable for the duties and responsibilities that the employee is being asked to fulfill. Such job postings are harming many organization's ability to fill their employment vacancies. Although everyone in an organization may not be a cybersecurity professional, all employees ought to be informed of their role in the cybersecurity structure of the organization. This technique leads to an increase in accountability for security incidents in the organization. As many organizations are using technology-based tools to combat cyberattacks in the place of larger cybersecurity teams, it has become necessary to use more preventative security practices based on an appropriately conducted risk assessments (DDLS Australia, 2019, p. 10). No cybersecurity plan is without vulnerabilities, but the use of proactive measures has the ability to minimize the risks and the need for reactive procedures. This can be achieved to continuous monitoring and conducting full security audits often. Organizations and their cybersecurity teams remain vigilant and protect their systems from cybersecurity threats that impact the three core principles: confidentiality, integrity, and availability (i.e., the *CIA triad*) of their systems.

Some of the cyber-skills gap can be decreased by promoting gender diversity and closing the gender wage gap. As stated above there many women that have the educational requirements and expertise to fill cybersecurity roles, but many of them feel like the "token" or misfit in their professional environment. Organizations need to do a better job of promoting inclusion in their workforce and improving their recruiting practices. According to Mohr (2018), studies have shown that most women will not apply for a role that they feel they do not meet 100% of the criteria for, whereas men will apply for roles if they meet at least 60% of the requirements. This practice results in a candidate pool that is overwhelmingly male. A way to combat this is by removing details from job announcements that are not actual requirements for the position the organization intends to fill.

As for recruiting practices, the requirements requested from the candidate pool need to be reasonable. It has been commonly reported by job seekers that the years of expertise for a tool or other forms of technology required in some job postings actually exceed the age of the technology for which it is requested. Actions like this help to contribute to the skills gap and cause employment opportunities to remain unfilled for extended periods of time. Those posting job requirements need to be aware of what is being asked of the job seeker. Vacancy postings should not be a document filled with requirements for every possible type of technological tool for a position that does not require it. Additionally, organizations need to learn how to leverage the soft skills of their employees. By doing so, organizations have the ability to manage more of their cybersecurity shortfalls. Equality should be treated with the upmost importance in all companies. Ignoring the gender issues in the organization has the ability to inhibit innovation and contribute to the decline of the candidate pool of cybersecurity professionals (Cobb, 2018). Organizations must actively work to confront and change gender stereotypes and biases in technology-based career paths. In turn the representation of females in science, technology, engineering, and mathematics (STEM) careers will increase and assist in closing the cybersecurity skills gap. Gender biases are not the only preconceived notions that should be addressed when hiring cybersecurity professionals. Additional demographics such as age and race should also be addressed to create the most inclusive environments.

Digital forensics and cyber-investigations are somewhat unique in how they are handled. This is determined by whether the investigation is corporate or tied to law enforcement. Corporate concerns for digital forensics are primarily based on the detection of vulnerabilities and risk prevention. On the other hand, law enforcement's focus is that of investigation, admissibility in court and the prosecution of the suspect. The evolution of cloud technology has created a need for cloud forensic analysis and investigative procedures. According to a State of the Cloud survey conducted in 2016, there are insufficient forensic tools available that can perform in cloud environment. This is mostly due to the inability to physically access evidence for collection (Baldwin, et al. 2018, p. 313). Some cloud environments only provide SaaS and PaaS which makes it impossible to collect log files for the systems and eliminates the standard practice of client-side collection that takes place in traditional environments. The volatile nature of cloud computing further complicates evidence collection by easily removing data due to a system shut down or restart (Baldwin, et al. 2018, p. 313). Another complication in cloud-based forensics investigations is the location in which the data center exists, as this can require assistance from the government and law enforcement organizations of other countries to perform evidence collection. Preservation of evidence and the documentation of analysis are vital for substantiating the legality of the method of collection and proving the execution of criminal activity (Baldwin, et al. 2018, p. 314). Methods for securing data that has been collected such as multifactor identification should be implemented during the performance of the investigation.

One suggestion for enabling better processing of cloud computing forensic investigations is for cloud service providers should integrate certified and credentialed digital forensics analysts and cyber-investigators into their workforce. By doing so CSPs have the ability to properly maintain and preserve that data being processed for investigations. Additionally, the possible implementation of an additional layer into the cloud computing environment such as a forensic server which could assist in conducting cyber-investigations and cloud forensics. In this server, system logs can be stored for virtual machines and will not be deleted by shutting down or restarting. The location of these logs and associated data files would be in an environment with limited accessibility which would allow for improved cloud forensics investigations and data analysis. Cyber-investigators could then access these files through the use of forensic tools with hash algorithms to provide proof of data security and encryption. This change would contribute to the security of the data and the investigative procedures. This addition to cloud environments would protect forensic data from the volatility of cloud computing environments and provide time and reasonable access for thorough investigative actions.

The healthcare industry has consistently become the target of cyberattacks through the use of malware and ransomware. This is partially due to their negligible cybersecurity practices. With security breaches such as the Anthem, Inc. hack in 2015, which resulted in the largest healthcare related hacking event compromising the personally identifiable information of approximately 80 million Americans, vulnerabilities and unmitigated risks exist as medical organizations frequently lack proper cybersecurity practices (McGee, 2017). It is no surprise that the increased use of internet connected medical devices leaves the healthcare industry more susceptible to hacking incidents. According to Imprivata (2016), over 80% of healthcare related organizations have reported that they have been compromised by some form of cyberattack. Most of these attacks were in the form of malware, ransomware, and phishing emails. Healthcare related organizations need to implement strong security frameworks such as the Common Security Framework (CSF) published by HITRUST, the Health Information Trust Alliance. This framework contains 14 control categories, with 49 control objectives, and 156 control specifications to create a more secure healthcare computing environment (HITRUST, 2020). Medical IoT devices have an anticipated annual growth of 27.6% through 2024 (Matthews, 2020). In 2011, a hacker by the name of Jay Radcliffe proved that he could remotely take control of his implanted insulin pump and showed that it was possible to alter the dosage to cause a lethal outcome. This hacking experiment was later echoed by another hacker that was able to do the same with a drug infusion pump (Jaret, 2018). The following year, a vulnerability in a pacemaker was revealed demonstrating the ability to send a lethal shock to the patient in which it was embedded. These revelations caused the Food and Drug Administration (FDA) to release policies on internet connected medical devices and the need for cybersecurity and protective measures (Jaret, 2018). Due to these findings, there needs to be more guidance for the implementation of cybersecurity policies for medical IoT devices. Cybersecurity practices for these devices could implement the use of artificial intelligence. It can be used to perform monitoring of the information flowing in and out each connected device. By doing so, the cybersecurity professional or team conducting the monitoring would receive notification of an attempted attack and prevent it in real time (Li et al., 2018). Also, these devices, associated software and networks need to undergo in-depth penetration testing before being released for widespread commercial usage. Additionally, the devices should be continuously monitored for any indications of hacking whether failed or successful. Once a vulnerability in an internet-connected medical device is discovered it should be reported to the manufacturer with suggestions for remediation. It is the responsibility of the manufacturer to update the device with security patches as needed. If this is not done within a reasonable amount of time, healthcare organizations should discontinue the use of the device in the best interest of their patients and system security.

FUTURE RESEARCH DIRECTIONS

As the cloud computing environment grows additional research on implementing cloud forensic investigation framework needs to be addressed. Additionally, a standard for evidence collection and retaining a proper chain of custody in each cloud model could be an area of focus. Currently, tools such as FTK, EnCase, Wireshark, Sleuthkit, and X-Ways are considered industry standard tools for Digital Forensics, but they lack the capabilities needed to perform well in cloud computing environments. Future research should take an in-depth look at optimizing these tools for cloud forensics usage. Continued development of cloud-based forensic analysis tools such as FROST has the ability to remove the need for a cloud service provider's assistance or interference in cloud computing forensic analysis. As cloud forensics grows, a clear code of ethics for conducting this form of cyber-investigations should be addressed. In addition to the code of ethics, standardized certification paths will need further research and development. Also, the research and development of rigorous testing procedures and vulnerability assessment standards for internet connected medical devices is another area for exploration because as it currently stands, it is an easy area to exploit. This exploitation does not only lie with the device, but with the protected health information (PHI) and personally identifiable information (PII) that can be accessed through its penetration.

CONCLUSION

In conclusion, the top trends outlined above shows that the field of cybersecurity will continue to evolve and as cybersecurity professionals, we must evolve with it. The subset of digital forensics and cyber-investigations will always require additional learning and analytical thinking as the demand for expertise continues to grow and the advancement of cloud computing persists. The rapid advancement of both medical technology and cybersecurity will only lead to a greater need for the implementation of proper security measures. Hackers will continue to conduct attacks in an attempt to access secured environments without being detected. These attacks will only continue to get more sophisticated in nature. The prevalence of cybercrimes and other forms of cyberattacks will not decrease. It is the job of the cybersecurity professionals and every employee in their organization to combat these risks by promoting the proper use of technology and a solid cybersecurity policy. These policies must include proper risk assessments, vulnerability testing and the continuous monitoring of their networks through the use of human interaction and technological tools. Technology has the ability to assist the world in all areas of life, but this reward does not without increased risks. A risk deemed negligible without proper assessment could be the area of exploitation that is used by hackers to create a larger fallout. Cybersecurity as a technological field is ever evolving. There will never come a time where its top trends and progression will not be important in a world of heavy technology usage. The need for organizations to keep pace with the rapid development of technology will continue for years to come. With dedication, conscious effort, and leveraging the skills and personnel available the current skills gap of cybersecurity professionals should not take upwards of twenty years to close. Cloud computing is quickly becoming the normal and forensic investigative procedures must shift with it. Though the probability of the fatal hacking of internet connected medical devices is currently low, concerns for the information security structure of many healthcare related organizations should be treated with a high level of importance. Resolution of these issues will remain an ongoing process much like the remedial nature of cybersecurity. Cybersecurity practices are administered as a flexible and scalable method of protection.

REFERENCES

Alex, M. E., & Kishore, R. (2017). Forensics framework for cloud computing. *Computers & Electrical Engineering, 60,* 193–205. https://doig.org/10.1016/j. compeleceng.2017.02.006

Australia, D. D. L. S. (2019). *Meeting Australia's cyber security challenge.* DDLS Australia. Retrieved July 28, 2020, from https://www.ddls.com.au/wp-content/uploads/2019/08/DDLS-ebook-August-2019-Final.pdf

Baldwin, J., Alhawi, O. M., Shaughnessy, S., Akinbi, A., & Dehghantanha, A. (2018). Emerging from the cloud: A bibliometric analysis of cloud forensics studies. *Advances in Information Security Cyber Threat Intelligence, 70,* 311–331. https://doig.org/10.1007/978-3-319-73951-9_16

Cobb, M. J. (2018). Plugging the skills gap: The vital role that women should play in cyber security. *Computer Fraud & Security, 2018*(1), 5–8. https://doig.org/10.1016/s1361-3723(18)30004-6

Dykstra, J., & Sherman, A. T. (2013). Design and implementation of FROST: Digital forensic tools for the OpenStack cloud computing platform. *Digital Investigation, 10*(Supplement), S87–S95. https://doi.org/10.1016/j.diin.2013.06.010

Griffin, T. (2020, May 21). *Cybersecurity trends in 2020 & the threats facing the industry.* Retrieved July 21, 2020, from https://blog.eccouncil.org/cybersecurity-trends-in-2020-the-threats-facing-the-industry/

Herman, M., Iorga, M., Landreville, N., Lee, R., Mishra, A., Sardinas, R., & Wang, Y. (2020, August). *NISTIR 8006: NIST Cloud Computing Forensic Science Challenges.* Retrieved September 6, 2020, from doi:10.6028/NIST.IR.8006

HITRUST Alliance. (2020, August). *Introduction to the HITRUST CSF.* https://hitrustalliance.net/content/uploads/CSFv9.4_Introduction.pdf

Imprivata. (2016, February 23). *Imprivata expands authentication platform to protect medical devices and remote access to patient information from hacking* [Press release]. Retrieved September 7, 2020, from https://www.imprivata.com/company/press/imprivata-expands-authentication-platform-protect-medical-devices-and-remote-access

Jaret, P. (2018, November 12). *Exposing vulnerabilities: How hackers could target your medical devices.* Retrieved July 28, 2020, from https://www.aamc.org/news-insights/exposing-vulnerabilities-how-hackers-could-target-your-medical-devices

Jones, M. (2020). Stress testing the skills gap. *Computer Fraud & Security, 2020*(5), 9–11. https://doig.org/10.1016/s1361-3723(20)30051-8

Li, S., Pilcher, C., & Gepford, J. (2018). Cybersecurity war: A new front—Hospitals need to be proactive to prevent hacks of connected medical devices. *Trustee, 71*(6), 16.

Matthews, K. (2020, January 2). *3 healthcare cybersecurity trends to watch in 2020*. Retrieved July 21, 2020, from https://hitconsultant.net/2020/01/02/3-healthcare-cybersecurity- trends-to-watch-in-2020/#.XxeK1J5KhPY

McGee, M., & Ross, R. (2017, January 10). *A new in-depth analysis of Anthem breach*. Retrieved September 7, 2020, from https://www.bankinfosecurity.com/new-in-depth-analysis-anthem-breach-a-9627

Mohr, T. (2018, March 2). *Why women don't apply for jobs unless they're 100% qualified*. Retrieved September 17, 2020, from https://hbr.org/2014/08/why-women-dont-apply-for-jobs-unless-theyre-100-qualified

NAICS Code 541513: Computer facilities management services. (n.d.). Retrieved July 21, 2020, from https://www.naics.com/naics-code-description/?code=541513

Seigfried-Spellar, K. C., Rogers, M. K., & Crimmins, D. M. (2017). Development of a professional code of ethics in digital forensics. In *Proceedings of the Conference on Digital Forensics, Security & Law* (pp. 135–144). Academic Press.

Standard Occupational Classification System. (2020, April 17). Retrieved July 21, 2020, from https://www.bls.gov/soc/2018/major_groups.htm#15-0000

ADDITIONAL READING

Caldwell, T. (2013). Plugging the cyber-security skills gap. *Computer Fraud & Security, 2013*(7), 5–10. doi:10.1016/S1361-3723(13)70062-9

SME Channels. (2019, April 15). *Fortinet continues commitment to close the cyber skills gap through its NSE Institute training and certification program*. Author.

Everett, C. (2020). Act now to solve the cyber skills gap: The UK government is attempting to address the lack of skills in the cyber security space—but should it be doing more? *Computer Weekly, 21*, 21–25.

Herman, M., & Iorga, M. (2016, August 31). *NIST cloud computing forensic science*. Retrieved September 6, 2020, from https://www.nist.gov/programs-projects/nist-cloud-computing-forensic-science

Infosec. (n.d.). *Computer forensics certifications*. Retrieved September 6, 2020, from https://resources.infosecinstitute.com/category/computerforensics/introduction/computer-forensics-certifications/

Jones, S. (2018). Protecting medical devices from hackers. *Electronics World, 124*(1988), 30–32.

Legal Monitor Worldwide. (2020, March 16). *Cyber security skills gap: Useless certs, too few women, poor training*. Author.

Manoj, S. K. A., & Bhaskari, D. L. (2016). Cloud forensics: A framework for investigating cyber attacks in cloud environment. *Procedia Computer Science, 85*, 149–154. doi:10.1016/j.procs.2016.05.202

Manral, B., Somani, G., Choo, K.-K. R., Conti, M., & Gaur, M. S. (2020). A systematic survey on cloud forensics challenges, solutions, and future directions. *ACM Computing Surveys, 52*(6), 1–38. doi:10.1145/3361216

Roussev, V., Ahmed, I., Barreto, A., McCulley, S., & Shanmughan, V. (2016). Cloud forensics: Tool development studies & future outlook. *Digital Investigation, 18*, 79–95. doi:10.1016/j.diin.2016.05.001

Simou, S., Kalloniatis, C., Gritzalis, S., & Katos, V. (2019). A framework for designing cloud forensic-enabled services (CFeS). *Requirements Engineering, 24*(3), 403–430. doi:10.100700766-018-0289-y

Tenders Info News. (2020, August 26). *United States: Check Point Software partners with Harvard and MIT-founded edX to Deliver Free Online Courses, to help close cyber-security skills gap*. Author.

KEY TERMS AND DEFINITIONS

Cloud Investigation Framework: A collection of standards and processes to aid in the performance of cloud forensic investigations.

Cloud Service Provider: A company or organization who provides cloud-based products and infrastructure.

Cross-Border Law: Laws that enable investigations to be conducted in different jurisdictions with the help of other governments.

Digital Forensics: The process of recovering and investigating the data stored on digital devices such as computers and mobile phones.

Firewall: Hardware or software solutions used to prevent unauthorized access to private networks through the internet.

Gender Wage Gap: The difference in earnings between men and women. This amount varies by education and other demographics.

Intrusion Detection System: A device or software solution that monitors networks and systems for malicious activity.

Junk Science: Scientific information deemed faulty or biased to provide intentional results.

Multi-Tenancy: Architecture and software that is hosted to serve multiple organizations using the same pool of resources.

Virtual Machine: A computer instance that uses software instead of hardware to run programs and applications.

Chapter 7

Emerging Trends in the Mitigation of Data Security of Consumer Devices Industry

Alusine Jalloh
University of Maryland Global Campus, USA

ABSTRACT

Previous literature has investigated if mobile applications unregulated by the United States, such as Tik-Tok, can have a detrimental impact regarding the vulnerability of personal identifiable information of their daily users and are therefore worthy of banned designation for consumer use in the United States. The research conducted in these findings aimed to assess the benefits and downsides of user-permitted data collection from mobile applications such as Tik-Tok including whether Tik-Tok indeed poses a serious national security threat due to its potential exploitation from foreign governments, therefore warranting government escalation from being closely monitored to banned status. This chapter's research also consisted of analyzing emerging trends in the mitigation of data security of consumer devices industry in the instances of cloud computing, 5G implementation in home automation, and mobile applications privacy. Previous findings implicate the potential vulnerability of PII in mobile applications and support the notion of Tik-Tok becoming banned by the United States.

DOI: 10.4018/978-1-7998-6504-9.ch007

CLOUD COMPUTING

Cloud computing has become a common mechanism allowing users to enjoy increased functionality for productivity and allocate important information for flexibility in managing and sharing data. By accepting terms and conditions from cloud providers, users must inherently trust that their information is being kept safe while still acknowledging that they are responsible for any of the outcomes involved in information stored on the cloud were to become compromised. Many cybersecurity experts recognize that cloud configurations are often targeted by hackers or persons with dubious intent to steal personal or private data as well as gain access to credentials.

Cloud computing is often featured in three distinct forms such as Infrastructure as a service (IaaS), Platform as service (PaaS), and Software as a service (SaaS). Regarding the mitigation of data security risks in the industry of consumer devices, all three variations of cloud computing involve third-party vendors handling virtualization, networking, storage, and server maintenance. With that in mind cloud computing can be prone to class break vulnerability due to misconfiguration from users. Arce sheds light on an instance in which "during the summer of 2019, a former AWS employee exploited a misconfigured Capital One server to obtain the credentials needed to steal 106 million Capital One records stored on AWS" (Arce, 2020, p.4). With cloud computing, scenarios like the one aforementioned are expected as indirect risks arise during the process when developers of products and services become connected with users through exchanges within cloud computing. Arce touches on this concept by divulging that "cloud services providers create *indirect externalities* in that the value of the CSP for those on one side of the market rises with increased participation on the other side of the market" (Arce, 2020, p.5) and also points out that the cloud exchange markets are plagued by individuals such as hackers with the sole intent of commandeering vulnerabilities in cloud services for malicious uses.

The reputation of cloud-based providers (CSP) in mitigating exploitation and responding resoundingly to threats is paramount for their value perceived by consumer users. Within PaaS, CSPs are responsible for the security of API, in SaaS cloud architecture is the responsibility of CSPs, and in IaaS the hypervisor is the liability of the CSP. The variability in responsibility in the different cloud computing models demonstrates the shared liability model in cloud adoption by consumer users. Acre characterizes the properties of *cybersecurity symbiosis* within the growing trend of cloud computing as an inverse relationship in which competition between CSPs influences cybersecurity and cybersecurity shapes competition between CSPs. (Acre, 2020)

5G Implementation in Home Automation

Smart home technology is a case-in-point example of double-edge sword technology designed for the key purpose of making life easier also having the potential to expose users to risks and vulnerabilities that are often incommensurate with the benefits that are provided. While home automation has been trending for several decades, the recent push for the widespread rollout of 5G technology has bolstered the efficiency of several appliances all working together and communicating with each other as a system inside a domicile, hence increasing the drive for advancements in home automation. 5G wireless sensor networks are typically susceptible to active and passive attacks by hackers who wish to attempt a modification of data, impersonation of user credentials, replay data, and eavesdrop to gain private and personal information (Al-Muhtadi, 2019). In the case of integration of home automation, there is an increased list of negative outcomes if the privacy and security of smart home appliances are compromised.

Optimization of smart homes depends on direct to direct communication of appliances in real-time that share information and network connectivity with low latency found in 5G enabled internet-of-things efficiency. Home automation that ideally features an omnipresent state of network connectivity can be achieved by 5G, which is capable of decreasing latency up to 100 times when compared to its predecessor 4G and is thus more apt to achieve much higher availability. (Mistry, 2020). Home automation that utilizes blockchain with internet-of-things services of appliances has the added benefit of mitigating data compromises from middle-man-attacks since it eliminates the involvement of a third party when sharing data through peer-to-peer communications. (Mistry, 2020)

The scalability of home automation provided by 5G high-speed connectivity stems from the ability to overcome high bandwidth capacity limitations required by numerous sensors of multiple devices connected on the same network. Smart home automation and participating devices are designed to improve the quality of life of users in real-time by providing "security, convenience, and comfort to the owners, by allowing them to control the settings according to their preference with the help of smartphone applications." (Mistry, 2020, p. 6) The long list of smart home appliances are still growing, however, some numerous examples of home automation applications include smart home surveillance, smart doors with remote lock mechanisms, smart thermostats that adjust based to preset preferences and identified presence of occupants in the home, voice-controlled smart-cooking that activates kitchen appliances, and smart lighting that like smart-thermostats can change on demand or respond to preset preferences based on the time of the day or outdoor lighting. The most potentially challenging adverse outcome of the smart home automation involves unauthorized access and subsequent intrusion of the smart door lock system by intruders who intend to circumvent the authentication of the smart door lock system to compromise security. (Mistry, 2020) The low latency provided by 5G networks takes many steps in mitigating data compromise by detecting and preventing intrusion with the use of multiple sensors in real-time, working together with a blockchain-based lock system to block unauthorized open/lock commands from finding success.

Mobile Applications

Security breaches of a mobile application operating systems on consumer devices are one of the most pervasive and prevalent types of cybersecurity vulnerability in the industry today. A larger percentage of the United States population depends on the daily access to services provided by mobile consumer devices like phones/tablets/smart-watches as opposed to stationary-device cloud computing or even smart home automation. By utilizing mobile applications, smartphone or tablet users can enjoy the added convenience of activities such as traveling more efficiently with the use of location services, and accessing centralized systems at moment's notice like mobile bank accounts, or monitoring and uploading their personal information onto social media accounts while engaging with friends, family, associates, and strangers from across the world in real-time.

Proximity-based applications that capitalize on location-based social network discovery or ridesharing, are classic examples of mobile applications that can expose users to privacy and security vulnerability. Vulnerabilities can occur in the form of location leaks when the estimated location of the consumer is uploaded to the mobile application's dedicated coordinate servers. An even greater risk is the inherent design of rideshare applications that ask for the input of the consumer to provide exact "user ID, departure time, departure place, and destination place from passengers are transmitted to the app server" (Shuang, 2018, p. 2) that is then broadcasted to all nearby available drivers. Past research has shown location-based parameters can be intercepted and tampered with by individuals wishing to bypass standard limitations and spoof location to request access to services or individuals anywhere through geocoordinate extraction. The trend of proximity-based applications is already prominent and still growing in popularity. For example, WeChat has over 540 million worldwide active users monthly, while Didi, the largest ridesharing app in china currently enjoys more than 300 million unique consumers. (Shuang, 2018). Concerning risk evaluations and the mitigation of data leakage in Chinese proximity-based apps such as WeChat, Weibo, Didi Momo, and Mitalk, previous research by Shuang has found their privacy protection to be insufficient as they possess a high risk of location data leakage. Next, I will delve into a very controversial, Chinese social media app by the name of Tik-Tok and its emerging narrative in the United States that might lead to its ban as an extreme countermeasure.

An Emerging Issue in Mobile Application Security, Tik-Tok Data Controversy

Tik-Tok is a popular video-sharing application, with over one billion users, that is currently experiencing intense observation and scrutiny from the US government based on suspicions that its data vulnerabilities might be exploited by or exposed to the Chinese government intelligence. Previous research conducted by the security company Check Point Research has uncovered numerous vulnerabilities within the app including the possibility of "the ability to take partial control of other users' accounts, including the ability to delete and upload videos and make hidden videos public: spoofing SMS messages to users as though they are coming from Tik-Tok; and obtaining users personal information" (Bunker, 2020, p. 19). Tik-Tok has since patched the issues uncovered by Check Point Research but the apprehension remains that while a specific attack method most likely additional potential areas of vulnerabilities were discovered and patched, there may be other yet to be discovered types of threats that will allow a hacker to commodore the sensitive personal information stored within the application for nefarious uses. A more urgent concern that has emerged surrounding Tik-Tok, is its purchase by the Chinese company Bytedance, two years prior. Bytedance has been known to build technology responsible for "face-swapping on videos, essentially making it easy to create deep-fake videos" that can be used to spread misinformation. As a result, both the United States Navy and Army have already banned the app from being downloaded on government-issues devices due to concerns of possible espionage, and congressmen have expressed concerns that the app could be implemented in the upcoming campaign interference and influence. (Bunker, 2020) Tik-Tok functions as a mostly algorithm-driven social media app and therefore inherently depends on the collection of sensitive information like preferences and tendencies to create a more user-friendly experience. The platform has raised heightened concerns with US congress regarding its potential threat to national security, and the US Federal Trade Commission settled a complaint against Tik-Tok regarding the illegal collection from minors which eventually led to the drafting of the Children's' Online Privacy Protection Act. (Bunker, 2020)

In closing this chapter, it should be reiterated that vendors of consumer devices must go through great lengths to ensure that their services can detect and mitigate, the prevalence of data leaks regarding personal and private user data. Consumer device information can be susceptible in many areas due to functionalities in network communications, location-based tracking, and algorithm centered services. Previous research in the consumer devices trends of cloud computing, 5G home automation, and mobile applications have highlighted the potential of negative outcomes for users when these systems are compromised, and this chapter has particularly explored the implications of privacy risks through mobile apps similarly to Tik-Tok. Based on previous findings and measures, this chapter's author supports the growing stance that our United States government should proceed with banning the use and download of Tik-Tok on consumer devices as its vulnerabilities pose as a glaring national security risk.

REFERENCES

Al-Muhtadi, J., Shahzad, B., Saleem, K., Jameel, W., & Orgun, M. A. (2019). Cybersecurity and privacy issues for socially integrated mobile healthcare applications operating in a multi-cloud environment. *Health Informatics Journal*, *25*(2), 315–329. doi:10.1177/1460458217706184 PMID:28480788

Anderson, K. E. (2020). Getting acquainted with social networks and apps: It is time to talk about TikTok. *Library Hi Tech News*, *37*(4), 7–12. doi:10.1108/LHTN-01-2020-0001

Arce, D. G. (2020). Cybersecurity and platform competition in the cloud. *Computers & Security*, *93*, 101774. Advance online publication. doi:10.1016/j.cose.2020.101774

Bunker, G. (2020). Tik-Tok Danger. *Network Security*, *2020*(1), 3–3. doi:10.1016/S1353-4858(20)30004-0

Chen, S., Zhao, S., Han, B., & Wang, X. (2019). 2019 wireless days (wd). In Investigating and revealing privacy leaks in mobile application traffic (pp. 1–4). IEEE. doi:10.1109/WD.2019.8734246

Choo, K.-K. R., Bishop, M., Glisson, W., & Nance, K. (2018). Internet- and cloud-of-things cybersecurity research challenges and advances. *Computers & Security*, *74*, 275–276. doi:10.1016/j.cose.2018.02.008

Faheem, K., & Rafique, K. (2015). Securing 4g/5g wireless networks. *Computer Fraud & Security*, *2015*(5), 8–12. doi:10.1016/S1361-3723(15)30036-1

Gupta, R., Tanwar, S., Tyagi, S., & Kumar, N. (2019). Tactile internet and its applications in 5g era: A comprehensive review. *International Journal of Communication Systems*, *32*(14), e3981. Advance online publication. doi:10.1002/dac.3981

Hong, J. B., Nhlabatsi, A., Kim, D. S., Hussein, A., Fetais, N., & Khan, K. M. (2019). Systematic identification of threats in the cloud: A survey. *Computer Networks*, *150*, 46–69. doi:10.1016/j.comnet.2018.12.009

Mistry, I., Tanwar, S., Tyagi, S., & Kumar, N. (2020). Blockchain for 5g-enabled iot for industrial automation: A systematic review, solutions, and challenges. *Mechanical Systems and Signal Processing*, *135*, 106382. Advance online publication. doi:10.1016/j.ymssp.2019.106382

Rao, S. K., & Prasad, R. (2018). Impact of 5g technologies on industry 4.0. *Wireless Personal Communications: An International Journal*, *100*(1), 145–159. doi:10.100711277-018-5615-7

Shuang, Z., Xiapu, L., Xiaobo, M., Bo, B., Yankang, Z., Wei, Z., ... Xinliang, Q. (2018). (2018). Exploiting proximity-based mobile apps for large-scale location privacy probing. *Security and Communication Networks*, *2018*, 1–22. Advance online publication. doi:10.1155/2018/3182402

Chapter 8
DWT–Based Steganography for Image Transmission

Sahar A. El-Rahman

Computer Science Department, Princess Nourah Bint Abdulrahman University, Riyadh, Saudi Arabia & Electrical Engineering Department, Benha University, Cairo, Egypt

ABSTRACT

Due to internet development, data transfer becomes faster and easier to transmit and receive different data types. The possibility of data loss or data modification by a third party is high. So, designing a model that allows stakeholders to share their data confidently over the internet is urgent. Steganography is a term used to hide information and an attempt to conceal the existence of embedded information in different types of multimedia. In this chapter, a steganography model is proposed to embed an image into a cover image based on DWT approach as the first phase. Then, the embedded secret image is extracted from the stego-image as the second phase. Model performance was evaluated based on signal noise ratio (SNR), PSNR, and MSE (mean square error). The proposed steganographic model based on DWT is implemented to hide confidential images about a nuclear reactor and military devices. The findings indicate that the proposed model provides a relatively high embedding payload with no visual distortion in the stego-image. It improves the security and maintains the hidden image correctness.

DOI: 10.4018/978-1-7998-6504-9.ch008

INTRODUCTION

Nowadays, Technology and Digital Communication are changing society's daily routine by using the data in different ways in life, and this using effect on the economic and the social. After the quick growth of the internet and mobile network, these days, we can see smaller devices with high performance and this technology never stops, which will help develop more ideas to help us in the future (Bucerzan et al., 2013). In the technology revolution, we use computers to save the data as digital forms, and the internet helps to transfer digital data between devices—the internet as it is open for everyone and made our lives easier. Also, there are many risks with using it. Some data we want to keep it secret, but some hackers want to see and change some data illegally. For that information security starts to be critical and a major in many institutions (Chen & JuLin, 2006). The way of embedding a confidential message in media (audio, text, image, and video) without change in the host signal, and one of the essential ways to hide information is Steganography that means "Covered Writing" in Greek (Abdelwahab & Hassaan, 2008). The other way to hide information is Cryptography, which provides a way of securing a reliable connection. Steganography has many algorithms not just for having a secret message, but also to have a correct message. It secures the information to have a secure connection (Vijay & Vigneshkumar, 2013). The big problem with Cryptography is the secure message is clear. Anyone can see the message when it is transmitted, which makes it less secure than Steganography, which is more secure in hiding information when we compare them (Kumar & Kumar, 2010). Using Steganography is to bypass the worry of hidden message (Narasimmalou & Joseph, 2012).

BACKGROUND

Data Hiding

This technology utilizes to hide secret messages (Kumar & Pooja, 2010). The types of security system are two different types Cryptography and Steganography. Cryptography is a set of two Greek words Crypto means "Secret" and Graphy means "writing" is a way to changing the message to another secret form is differ style the original with the support of a secret key and this process is called Encryption. Use Cryptography to refer to the science and art of transforming messages to make them secure to attacks. Changed value of the secret message called cipher and to get the original message from cipher called Decryption (Kumar, 2014). There are two types of information hiding; the first is watermarking technology embeds a message into an image, text, or other digital objects (Nasereddin, 2011). Steganography is considered as the art and science of communicating in a way that hides the presence of communication. The goal to hide messages inside other messages in a way does not allow any scamper even to detect that there is a second message existing (Thampi, 2004). Steganography in the security domain as shown in Figure 1 (Sumathi et al., 2014), and the cryptography, watermarking, and steganography comparison as indicated in Table 1 (Kumar, 2014).

The steganographic system embeds hidden content in unremarkable cover media (Provos & Honeyman, 2003). Steganography word of two Greek words "stegos" and "grafia". Stego means "cover" and grafia means "writing". Steganalysis is a technique to uncover the presence of steganography. Steganography is the practice of embedding secret information in a way such that the existence of the information hides. The original file referred to as cover text, cover image, or cover audio. The secret message referred to a stego-object after inserting. To enclose the extraction or detection of the embedded data, a stego-key will be used for hiding (Kumar, 2014).

Figure 1. Steganography in the security domain.
Source: (Sumathi et al., 2014)

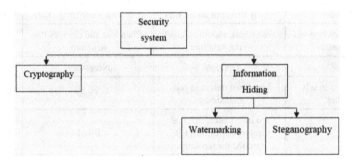

Steganography in Digital Media

- **Video or Audio steganography**: The secret messages hidden in video or audio files. The binary sequence of audio/video files differs slightly from the original file and cannot easily be detected by the eye. Some types of video or audio steganography are Echo hiding, Phase coding, Spread Spectrum (Kumar, 2014).

- **Text steganography**: This type of steganography hides a secret message in a text. Many techniques are used sequencing in each character of the secret messages. They hid a fixed position or the binary value of the secret message (Kumar, 2014).

- **Image steganography**: This technique exploits a weakness of the human visual system (HVS). HVS cannot detect the variation in luminance of color vectors at the combination of color pixels. The single pixels can be represented by their optical higher frequency side of the visual spectrum. A picture represented by characteristics like 'brightness', 'chroma'. These characteristics can be expressed in terms of 1sand 0s. If the terminal receiver of the data is nothing but the human visual system (HVS) then use the Least Significant Bit (LSB) for something other than color information (Doshi et al., 2012; Sheth & Tank, 2015).

- **Protocol Steganography**: Embedding information inside messages and network control protocols used in network transmission. In the layers of OSI network, the covert channels can be used in the steganography (Kumar, 2014).

Table 1. Comparison of Cryptography, Watermarking, and Steganography.

Steganography	Watermarking	Cryptography	
Digital media.	Mostly image or audio files.	Text with some image files.	**Carrier**
Payload and no changes to the structure.	Watermark and no changes to the structure.	Plain text and changes the structure.	**Secret data**
Optional.	Optional.	Necessary.	**Key**
Least two unless in self-embedding.	Least two unless in self-embedding.	One.	**Input files**
Blind.	An informative original watermark or cover is needed for recovery.	Blind.	**Detection**
Full retrieval data.	By cross correlation.	Full retrieval data.	**Authentication**
Secret communication.	Copyright preserving.	Data protection.	**Objective**
Stego-file.	Watermarked-file.	Cipher-text.	**Result**
Delectability/ capacity.	Robustness.	Robustness.	**Concern**
Steganalysis.	Image processing.	Cryptanalysis.	**Type of attacks**
Never.	Sometimes.	Always.	**Visibility**
Detected.	Removed or replaced.	De-ciphered.	**Fails when**
The message is more important than the cover.	The cover is more important than the message.	N/A.	**Relation to cover**
Choose any appropriate cover.	Cover is restricted.	N/A.	**Flexibility**
Ancient except digital version.	Modern.	Modern.	**History**

Source: (Kumar, 2014)

- **DNA Steganography**: DNA Steganography is a cutting edge technology in this domain. It based on the characteristics of natural DNA sequences in the cell. Where, in molecular biology, the deoxyribonucleic acid will be utilized to store the genetic information, known as DNA in the cells. Four nucleotides make DNA, which are Thymine (T), Cytosine (C), Guanine (G), and Adenine (A). These bases connected by a backbone of DNA strands that consider these sugar components and phosphate groups, identifying this backbone the direction of the DNA strands (Mousa et al., 2011; Kumarpanjabi & Singh, 2013); Mitras & Aboo, 2013).

STEGANOGRAPHY TECHNIQUES

Spatial Domain

Techniques using the pixel gray levels and their color values directly for encoding the message bits. These techniques are considered the simplest schemes in the complexity of embedding and extraction. The drawback of these methods is the amount of additive noise that creeps in the image directly affects the Peak Signal to Noise Ratio and the statistical Characteristics of the image. These embedding algorithms are applicable mainly to lossless image-compression schemes such as TIFF images. For lossy-compression schemes such as JPEG, the message bits get lost during the compression step (Sravanthi et al., 2012). Directly, some bits in the image pixel values will be modified by the hiding data. LSB (Least significant bit) is the simplest common approach that is used to embed a secret message in the LSB of pixel without introducing many perceptible distortions. The modifications in a value of the pixel LSB will be unnoticeable for visual human system (Hussain, 2013). The most steganography approaches in spatial domain are:

- **LSB:** the advantages of this approach are the original image degradation is with the minimal chance. Lot of information can be stored in an image. But this approach has some drawbacks that it is not strong, due to the hidden message can be lost in the processing of the image, and also the simple attacks can demolish the embedded message (Hussain, 2013).
- **PVD (Pixel value differencing):** Gray scale image as a cover image with a long bit-stream as the secret data. The cover is divided into no overlapping blocks of two pixels, pi and pi+1 each block difference value di is by subtracting pi from pi+1. The set of all different values might range from -255 to 255 (Mandal, 2012).

- **EBE (Edges Based data embedding):** Hide secret data into the pixels that make up the extracted edges of the carrier image. The secret data can be of any type and embedded into the three pixel LSBs of the carrier image, but not in each pixel, only in the ones that are the section of the edges detected by the edge detection algorithm (Tiwari et al., 2014).

- **RPE (Random Pixel Embedding):** Data is hidden in some randomly been chosen pixel. Random pixel created by using a Fibonacci algorithm (Tiwari et al., 2014).

- **Connectivity or Labeling approach:** A morphological processing starts in the peaks in the marker image and spreads throughout the rest of the image based on the pixels connectivity. Connector knows pixels are connected to other pixels. A set of pixels that connected based on Connectivity types, called an Object (Tiwari et al., 2014).

- **Pixel-intensity based approach:** The three color sailplanes converted into binary values. For every pixel in the image the plane has the minimal number of ones in its MSB will act as index plane and the other two color planes are considered as data plans (Shobana & Manikandan, 2013).

- **Texture-based approach:** The secret and host images are divided to blocks of a specific size and every block in a secret image taken as a texture pattern for which the most similar block found between the blocks of the host image. Embedding procedure is carried on by replacing small blocks of the secret image with blocks in the host image in like a way that least distortion (Tiwari et al., 2014).

- **Shifting the histogram approach:** A histogram of the image employed for finding the gray surfaces of the pixels of the cover image, every of which pixels covers one bit of the encrypted data (Koochaksaraei et al., 2012).

Transform Domain

Different transformations and techniques are utilized to hide the confidential data in the cover media. The embedding process of a message in the frequency domain is considered powerful than embedding methods that are utilized in the time domain. Most of the strongest steganographic systems operate within the Transform domain techniques have a feature over spatial domain techniques as they hide the message in the image regions that are less revealed to the cropping, compression, and image processing (Hussain, 2013). Hiding data in mathematical functions in compression algorithms. DCT technique used to transform domain algorithms for expressing a waveform as a weighted total of cosines. The data is hidden in the image by altering the DCT coefficient of the image. DCT coefficients fall below a specific threshold are exchanged with the secret bits. Taking the inverse transform will supply the stego-image. The extraction procedure consists in recovering those specific DCT coefficients (Kumar, 2014).

- **DFT (Discrete Fourier transformation):** it is the transform that deals with a limited discrete time signal and a limited or a discrete recurrences number. In the case of discrete time signals, the Discrete Fourier Transform (DFT) is openly used for ghostly analysis. The recurrences of the coordinated in the DFT usually depend on the extent of the convert, N, and they are integer double of the primary recurrence $\Delta f = \dfrac{f_s}{N}$, where fs clarify the sampling recurrence. Also, Δf give the recurrence resolution of the DFT. In this case, when the transform extent N is not a double of the signal time, the signal is a sum of coordinated components whose recurrence are not acting in the N-point DFT chain by a single spectral line- this impact is called "Leakage" into the contiguous DFT spectral coefficients set at the integer multiples of Δf (Sysel & Rajmic, 2012).

- **Fast Fourier transformation technique (FFT):** The Fast Fourier Transformation (FFT) is an algorithm for computing DFT, the purpose of presenting FFT is the request to minimize complication. Time and cost of DFT lowering is done by simulating that N is an integer, double of 2. There are different techniques including the radix-2, radix-4, split radix, Win grad, and major factor algorithms that are used for computing the DFT. These algorithms are pointed to as the fast Fourier Transform (FFT) algorithms. Now, we are explaining the radix-2 decimation-in-time FFT algorithm. To provide a public frame of reference, we can count the computational complication of the immediate implementation of the K-point DFT for the time-limited sequence *x[k]* with extensive K. Depend on its definition, as shown in Table 2 (Smith, 1999). Illustration of the four Fourier transforms. A signal may be continuous or discrete, and it may be periodic or aperiodic. Together these define four possible combinations, each having its own version of the Fourier transform. The names are not well organized; simply memorize them (Smith, 1999).

- **DCT (Discrete Cosine Transformation):** it is used for the compression of image where acceptable regression is happening. When we are using the computer for different purpose and most our work on the computer, we need for huge hard-disk and moving data between devices. Choosing the best way of saving data is important. As we live in fast live and developing technology faster, we are in the digital world. Now, we can find any information as digital by using the internet and those huge information on the internet usually are not secure and anyone can change it or rewrite it as he/she wants.

Image compression is minimizing its size, but it will change the quality of the image to an acceptable quality. Reducing the size of the image will allow us to store more images. Also, it will minimize the time for sending the image by using the internet to other devices. JPEG and JPEG 2000 are two important techniques used for image compression (Gautam, 2010). The Discrete Cosine Transform (DCT) is a technique for transferring a signal into primary recurrence components. It is usually utilized with the compression of the image. There are some functions are used to compute the DCT and to compress images. These functions explain the power of mathematics in the prototyping of image processing algorithms (Watson, 1994). JPEG image compression usually uses DCT. It is fast transforming and most used and powerful method for image compression. It has a prime compacting for highly reconditioned data. DCT has fixed ground images and gives adjustment between information packing capability and computational complication. JPEG 2000 image compression usually uses DWT. It can be used to minimize the image size without affecting a lot on the resolutions computed and values less than a pre-specified beginning are ignored. It minimizes the size of memory utilized (Gautam, 2010).

Table 2. Transform Types

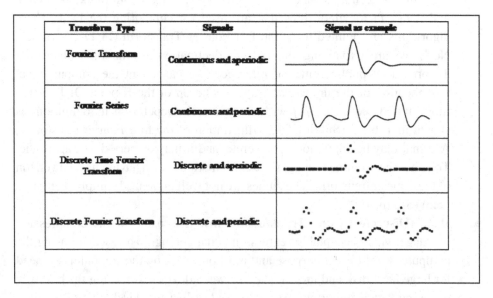

Transform Type	Signals	Signal as example
Fourier Transform	Continuous and aperiodic	
Fourier Series	Continuous and periodic	
Discrete Time Fourier Transform	Discrete and aperiodic	
Discrete Fourier Transform	Discrete and periodic	

- **WT (Wavelet Transform):** Wavelets are functions that provide succinct careful representations of time chain and orders of locative data. Wavelet

Transforms are the components of the wavelet domain. These transforms produce a strong tool that support analyzing the original domain. The water mark in this technique is embedded using separated wavelet transform DWT, which breaks up the image into three different resolutions and each part can be refined to make different scale decompositions. The watermark is embedded in high resolution which adds power and strength to it (Nasereddin, 2011).

- **DWT (Discrete Wavelet Transform):** DWT is a linear transformation that operates on a data vector whose extent is integer strength of two. It is transformed into a numerically different vector of the same extent. It is a tool for separates data into different recurrence components. After that, studies each component with a resolution matched to its weight. DWT is computed with a cascade of closeout, followed by a factor 2 subsampling as indicated in Figure 2. H and L denote high and low pass filters respectively, $\downarrow$ 2 denotes subsampling (Kociołek et al., 2001).

Figure 2. DWT Tree.
Source: *(Kociołek et al., 2001)*

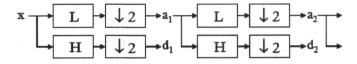

DFT and DCT are perfect frame, transform and any change in the transform coefficients affects the whole image unless if DCT is implemented by using a block based way. DWT has recurrence locality which means if the signal is embedded it will impact the image locally. Wavelet transforms provides both recurrence and spatial detailing for the image (Abdelwahab, & Hassaan, 2008). DWT is used for digital images. Different DWT is available based on the implementation time when should be used the easiest one is her transform. If you want to hide text message integer, we can use wavelet transform. When DWT is used in an image, it is separated to 4 sub-bands: LL, HL, LH, and HH. LL part contains the important features. If the data is hidden by LL part, the image can resist the compression. Sometimes deformation may be produced in the image and then other sub-bands can be used as shown in Figure 3 (Hemalatha et al., 2013). The four different sub-images are (Abdelwahab, & Hassaan, 2008):

- **LL:** unpolished almost as the original image containing the whole data about the image. It is gained by applying the low-pass filter on both x and y coordinates.
- **HL and LH:** they are both gained by applying the high-pass filter on one coordinate and the low-pass filter on the other one.
- **HH:** disable the high recurrence component of the image in the slanted direction. It is gained by applying the high-pass filter on both x and y coordinates. While human eyes are more sensitive to the low frequency part, LL is the important component in the reconstruction process.

Figure 3. Three Phase Decomposition Using DWT.
Source: (Parul et al., 2014)

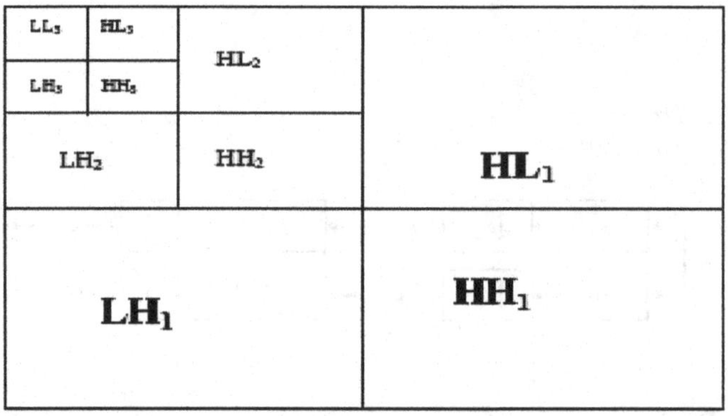

RELATED WORKS

Badescu & Dumitrescu (2014) proposed a new approach in this system has been used algorithm to hide information hide a secret message in small image size use Least Significant Bit (LSB) substitution and for hiding the image in the image cover use the DWT method. Message with a the length of 10,000 characters in a small 640 x 480 image grayscale result hides in an image of size 1024x1024. Abdelwahab & Hassaan (2008) proposed an algorithm based on DWT to hide a secret image inside a cover image by using two secret keys to obtain a stego-image. In this system proposed technique does not require the original cover image to extract the embedded secret image. Narasimmalou & Joseph (2012) proposed based on DWT in two different techniques. The first technique is performed by using three-level wavelet decomposition taking a single plane of the cover image for embedding and another technique is using single level wavelet decomposition.

PROPOSED MODEL

DWT transform the signal or data from one domain (spatial) to another domain (frequency) (Mstafa & Bac, 2013). DWT in the image processing is to multi-differentiated decomposing image into a sub image of different spatial domain. Transform coefficient of sub image after original image has been DWT transformed (Maharjan, & Qiaolun, 2014). When DWT is applied the image it is decomposed into 4 sub-bands {Low Low (LL), High Low (HL), Low High (LH) and High High (HH)}. Low frequency is known as the approximation sub image because it contains the same of the original signal. The other parts are more details of the signal they are not exact data as the original one (Mstafa & Bac, 2013).The HL, LH, HH sub-bands is the detail sub images containing the horizontal, vertical and diagonal details (Badescu, & Dumitrescu, 2014). So, if the information is hidden in LL part the image can be compressed or any other manipulations, but sometimes resulting in deformation of the image and then another sub band can be used (Hemalatha et al., 2013). The decomposition of the image with 2 levels of 2D- DWT is shown in Figure 4. A two-dimensional image after three-times DWT decomposed can be shown as Figure 5.

Figure 4. Levels of 2D – DWT.
Source: (Costa & Guedes, 2012)

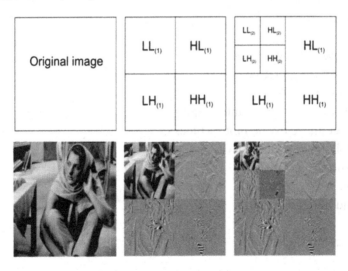

Figure 5. Three-times DWT decomposed.
Source: (Mishra et al., 2014)

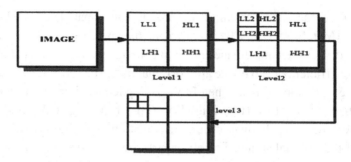

Haar Wavelets

The first DWT was invented by Hungarian mathematician Alfréd Haar. For an input represented by a list of 2^n numbers, the Haar wavelet transform may be considered to pair up input values, storing the difference and passing the sum. This process is repeated recursively, pairing up the sums to provide the next scale, which leads to 2^n-1 differences and a final sum. It is an example on DWT (Kumar, 2014).

Embedding Procedure and Extraction Procedure

Embedding Procedure

Step 1: Choose the cover image.
Step 2: Choose the secret image.
Step 3: Apply Haar-DWT.
Step 4: Cover image divided into 4 blocks.
Step 5: Secret image divided into 4 blocks.
Step 6: Apply Inverse Haar-DWT.
Step 7: Display stego-image.
Step 8: Save.
Step 9: Send it to the sender.

Extraction Procedure

Step 1: Choose the stego-image.
Step 2: Apply Haar-DWT.
Step 3: Stego-image divided into 4 blocks.
Step 4: Apply Inverse Haar-DWT.

Step 5: Display secret image.
Step 6: Save.

Implementation Details

Data implementation in the proposed model using DWT technique as beginning by importing the image wants to hide it (a secret image) and import cover image wants to hide secret image inside it .After import a cover image and the image's secret are divided into 4 sections (LL.LH, HH, HL) calls a function DWT. Then, calling the scale function to calculate the low and high frequencies for getting the best waves and frequencies to cover all spectrums. After that divide the two images to basic pixel colors (red, green and blue) . Then apply inverse DHWT then be merged image pixel confidential and cover image with each other the process occurs embed and return stego-image. In Extract Operation after adding the stego-image called the function DHWT to split image into 4 basic (LL, LH, HH, HL). After that divide the image to basic pixel colors (red, green and blue). And it is extracted the secret image pixel from cover image and return the secret image.

EXPERIMENTAL RESULTS

This section shows the results of the experiments conducted to measure the performance of the proposed approach. The proposed approach of the image steganography is tested by taking different cover images of different sizes and hiding the same hidden message in some of them. In this paper, different images were used with different size and different message size for each image. For performance evaluation different images were set and in error analysis, the distortion can be measured by SNR, PSNR and MSE. All of the measures are applied for the DWT embedding processes and the findings that are found from these experiments can be summarized in the Table 3. The experimental findings indicate that the proposed approach achieves a relatively high embedding capacity with no visual distortion in the resultant stegoimage. This work also demonstrates the competitive performance of the proposed system in comparison with other systems.

CONCLUSION

The risks of unauthorized access to secret information are increasing every day with the development of new technologies. As a solution image steganography can be used to protect confidential data from being revealed by unintended receivers. The

Table 3. Testing Measurements.

Cover Image	Cover Image Type	Cover image size	Secret Image	Secret Image Type	Secret Image Size	Cover image after Embed
	GIF	512*512		JPEG	85*65	
				PNG	101*80	
				JPEG	123*80	
				JPEG	217*232	
	PNG	1024X1024		PNG	97*80	
				JPEG	178*283	
				JPEG	265*265	
				GIF	480*335	

continued on following page

Table 3. Continued

Cover Image	Cover Image Type	Cover Image Size	Secret Image	Secret Image Type	Secret Image Size	Cover Image after Embed	PSNR	MSE	SNR
	JPEG	1024*1024		JPEG	50*50		38.61	8.94	31.71
				GIF	500*393		35.26	19.34	28.36
				PNG	400*320		36.17	15.67	29.28
				JPEG	100*100		38.45	9.28	31.55
				JPEG	250*202		37.59	11.31	30.69

Cover Image	Cover Image Type	Cover image size	Secret Image	Secret Image Type	Secret Image Size	Cover image after Embed	PSNR	MSE	SNR
	JPEG	550*550		PNG	101*180		36.62	14.13	32.67
				GIF	50*60		36.99	12.98	32.44
	PNG	480*483		GIF	200*140		29.85	67.24	26.64
				JPEG	89*91		30.21	61.90	27.00
				PNG	101*80		30.21	61.93	27.00
				JPEG	139*80		30.13	63.10	26.91
	bmp	1024*1024		JPEG	275*183		34.88	21.10	29.87
				JPEG	121*80		35.44	18.55	30.43
				GIF	500*500		33.32	30.23	28.31

aim of image steganography in this work is hiding secret mage inside another image "cover image" in a way that does not allow anyone to detect their existence. The image stegnographic model is presented for embedding secret images (confidential images) in cover images. Whereas, the image is converted to the frequency domain based on DWT. After that, embedding process takes place and finally the image is turned back to the original domain. The experimental findings indicate that the proposed model extracts the hidden image correctly. The experimental findings indicate that the proposed tool achieves a relatively high embedding capacity with no visual distortion in the resultant stego-image.

ACKNOWLEDGMENT

The authors would like to thank all the participants involved in this work especially to Doa S. Alkhudairi, Ebtsam K. Alanzi, Abeer M. Alamri, Ashwaq A. Alshmrani, Basha F. Alsahli. This research received no specific grant from any funding agency in the public, commercial, or not-for-profit sectors.

REFERENCES

A. B. (1994). Image compression using the discrete cosine transform. *The Mathematica Journal*, *4*(1), 81–88.

Abdelwahab, A. A., & Hassaan, L. A. (2008). A discrete wavelet transform based technique for image data hiding. *2008 National Radio Science Conference*, *1*(1), 1-9. 10.1109/NRSC.2008.4542319

Badescu, I., & Dumitrescu, C. (2014). Steganography in image using discrete wavelet transformation. *Advances in Mathematical Models and Production Systems in Engineering*, *1*(313), 69–72.

Bucerzan, D., Raţiu, C., & Manolescu, M. (2013). SmartSteg: A new android based steganography application. *International Journal of Computers, Communications & Control*, *8*(5), 681. doi:10.15837/ijccc.2013.5.642

Chen, P.Y. & JuLin, H. (2006). A DWT based approach for image steganography. *International Journal of Applied Science and Engineering.*, *1*(1), 275–290.

Costa, D. G., & Guedes, L. A. (2012). A discrete wavelet transform (dwt)-based energy-efficient selective retransmission mechanism for wireless image sensor networks. *Journal of Sensor and Actuator Networks, 1*(3), 3–35. doi:10.3390/jsan1010003

Doshi, R., Jain, P., & Lalit Gupta, L. (2012). Steganography and its applications in security. *International Journal of Modern Engineering Research, 2*(6), 4635.

Gautam, B. (2010). *Image compression using discrete cosine transform & discrete wavelet transform*. Bachelor of Technology Degree in Computer Science and Engineering at the National Institute of Technology, Rourkela (Deemed University). http://ethesis.nitrkl.ac.in/1731/1/project.pdf

Hemalatha, S. (2013). A Secure Color Image Steganography in Transform Domain. *International Journal on Cryptography and Information Security, 3*(1), 17–24. doi:10.5121/ijcis.2013.3103

Hussain, M. (2013). A survey of image steganography techniques. *International Journal of Advanced Science and Technology, 54*, 116-117.

Kociołek, M., Materka, A., Strzelecki, M., & Szczypiński, P. (2001). Discrete wavelet transform – derived features for digital image texture analysis. *International Conference on Signals and Electronic Systems, 2*.

Koochaksaraei, R., Aghazarian, V., Haroonabadi, A. &Hedayati, A. (2012). A novel data hiding method by using chaotic map and histogram. *International Journal of Innovation, Management and Technology, 3*(5), 642.

Kumar, A., & Pooja, K. (2010). Steganography- a data hiding technique. *International Journal of Computer Applications, 9*(7), 1–2.

Kumar, S. (2014). *Image steganography using improved LSB and EXOR encryption algorithm*. dspace.thapar.edu

Kumar, V., & Kumar, D. (2010). Performance evaluation of DWT based image steganography. *2010 IEEE 2nd International Advance Computing Conference (IACC), 1*(1), 223-228. 10.1109/IADCC.2010.5423005

Kumarpanjabi, P., & Singh, P. (2013). *An* enhanced data hiding approach using pixel mapping method with optimal substitution approach. *International Journal of Computer Applications, 74*(10), PP. 38.

Maharjan, S. K., & Qiaolun, G. (2014). Information hiding using image decomposing. *International Journal of Scientific Research, 3*(3), 73–76.

Mandal, J. (2012). Colour image steganography based on pixel value differencing in spatial domain. *International Journal of Information Sciences and Techniques, 2*(4), 84.

Mishra, M., & Adhikary, M. C. (2014). Detection of clones in digital images. *International Journal of Computer Science and Business Informatics, 9*(1), 91–101.

Mitras, B. A., & Aboo, A. (2013). Proposed steganography approach using DNA properties. *International Journal of Information Technology and Business Management, 14*(1), 79.

Mousa, H., Moustafa, K., Abdel-Wahed, W., & Hadhoud, M. (2011). Data hiding based on contrast mapping using DNA medium. *The International Arab Journal of Information Technology, 8*(2), 148.

Mstafa, R., & Bac, C. (2013). Information hiding in images using steganography techniques. *ASEE Northeast Section Conference Norwich University, 1*(1), 1–8.

Narasimmalou, T., & Joseph, A. R. (2012). Discrete Wavelet Transform Based Steganography for Transmitting Images. *IEEE-International Conference on Advances In Engineering, Science And Management*, 370-375.

Nasereddin, H. O. (2011). Digital watermarking a technology overview. *IJRRAS, 6*(1), 89–91.

Parul, M., & Rohil, H. (2014). Optimized Image Steganography using Discrete Wavelet Transform (DWT). *International Journal of Recent Development in Engineering and Technology, 2*(2), 75–81.

Provos, N., & Honeyman, P. (2003). Hide and seek: An introduction to steganography. *IEEE Secur. Privacy Mag., 1*(3), 32–44. doi:10.1109/MSECP.2003.1203220

Sheth, R. K., & Tank, R. M. (2015). Image steganography techniques. *International Journal of Computational Engineering Science, 1*(1), 10–11.

Shobana, M., & Manikandan, R. (2013). Efficient method for hiding data by pixel intensity. *International Journal of Engineering and Technology, 5*(1), 75.

Smith, S. W. (1999). The discrete Fourier transform. *The Scientist and Engineer's Guide to Digital Signal Processing*, 145. https://www.dspguide.com/ch8.htm

Sravanthi, G.S., Devi, B.S., Riyazoddin, S.M., & Reddy, M. J. (2012). A spatial domain image steganography technique based on plane bit substitution method. *Global Journal of Computer Science and Technology Graphics & Vision, 12*, 2-3.

Sumathi, C.P., Santanam, T. & Umamaheswari, G. (2014). A study of various steganographic techniques used for information hiding. *International Journal of Computer Science & Engineering Survey, 4*(6), 10-11. 4. doi:10.5121/ijcses.2013.4602

Sysel, P., & Rajmic, P. (2012). Goertzel algorithm generalized to non-integer multiples of fundamental frequency. *EURASIP Journal on Advances in Signal Processing, 2012*(1), 1.

Thampi, S. M. (2004). Information hiding techniques: a tutorial review. ISTE-STTP on Network Security & Cryptography, LBSCE, 1-3.

Tiwari, A., Yadav, S. R., & Mittal, N.K. (2014). A review on different image steganography techniques. *International Journal of Engineering and Innovative Technology, 3*(7), 122.

Vijay, M., & Vigneshkumar, V. (2013). Image steganography algorithm based on Huffman encoding and transform domain method. *2013 Fifth International Conference on Advanced Computing (ICoAC)*, 517. 10.1109/ICoAC.2013.6922005

KEY TERMS AND DEFINITIONS

Cryptography: It provides a way of securing a reliable connection.

Data Hiding: This technology utilizes to hide secret messages.

DCT (Discrete Cosine Transformation): A technique used to transform domain algorithms for expressing a waveform as a weighted sum of cosines.

DFT (Discrete Fourier Transformation): It is the transform that deals with a limited discrete time signal and a limited or a discrete recurrences number.

DWT (Discrete Wavelet Transform): It is a linear transformation that operates on a data vector whose extent is integer strength of two.

Information Security: It starts to be critical and a major in many institutions.

RPE (Random Pixel Embedding): Data is hidden in some randomly been chosen pixel. Random pixel created by using a Fibonacci algorithm.

Steganography: It has many algorithms not just for having a secret message, but also to have a correct message. The way of embedding a confidential message in media (audio, text, image, video), without change in the host signal, and it is one of the essential ways to hide information.

Chapter 9

The Socio–Economic Impact of Identity Theft and Cybercrime:
Preventive Measures and Solutions

Nabie Y. Conteh
Southern University at New Orleans, USA

Quinnesha N. Staton
University of Maryland Global Campus, USA

ABSTRACT

The purpose of this chapter is to explore and address the socio-economic impact of identity thefts and cybercrime in general. The chapter will further explain the various ways employed in their implementation. The chapter will also put forward ways to prevent the threats and vulnerabilities of the attacks. The study will also recommend solutions to stop and/or mitigate the consequences of cyber-thefts. The study will define social engineering as well as provide various social engineering tactic. The chapter will also discuss the reasons for the rise in cybercrime. Such reasons will include financial gain, revenge, as well as non-financial gains. Also cited are examples that demonstrate the capabilities of cybercriminal. The chapter will also provide justification for the reasons behind the cumbersome task and failure in instituting a lasting solution to the criminal activities. Finally, this chapter will close with a conclusion on the economic implications of social engineering on the general cyberwar on cybercrime at the national and global levels.

DOI: 10.4018/978-1-7998-6504-9.ch009

1. INTRODUCTION

Cybercrime is a growth industry. The returns accrued by cybercrimes are great, and the risks are low for the criminals that commit them. It is estimated that the likely annual cost to the global economy from the perpetration of cybercrimes is more than $400 billion (McAfee, 2014).

A conservative estimate would be $375 billion in losses, whereas the maximum could be upwards of as $575 billion. Even the smallest of these numbers far surpasses the national income of most countries. Most governments and companies underestimate the threats posed by cybercrimes and the exponential rate of their growth (McAfee, 2014).

"In 1994, Anthony Zboralski, a French hacker called the FBI office in Washington pretending to be an FBI representative working at the US embassy in Paris. Zboralski was able to persuade the person on the phone to tell him how to connect to the FBI's phone conferencing system. In seven months, he ran up a phone bill to $250,000." (Allen, 2006). How vulnerable are you? If you were a victim of a social engineering attack, would you even know? There are countless stories of companies falling victim to sophisticated social engineering attacks by some of the best cybercriminals. The war against companies and cyberspace marches on. It is important for organizations to understand what social engineering is, the various types of social engineering attacks, the reason for the rise in cybercrime and its impact, and recommendations for preventative measures.

2. WHAT IS SOCIAL ENGINEERING?

- **The article "Social Engineering:** The Basics" (Goodchild, 2012) defines social engineering as being able to gaining access to property (buildings, systems or data) by exploiting the human psyche, rather than by breaking in or hacking. According to (Heary, n.d.), social engineering is defined as any act that influences a person to take an action that may or may not be in their best interest. But social engineering is much more than that. Social engineering focuses on the psychological, physiological and technological aspects of influencing people. There are several types of social engineering attacks and they continue to evolve daily. Examples of these types of attacks are:
- Familiarity Exploit: a person pretending to be an employee or a malicious employee trying to fit in and appear normal, to make everyone feel comfortable like they should be there. They make themselves familiar with those that they want to exploit. Unknowingly, that person lowers their guard, and eventually

falls prey to the attacker. People react differently to people that they know or that they have been around. An example would be a social engineer tailgating into a secure area behind someone that they have become familiar with (The official social engineering portal - security through education, 2015).

- **Reading Body Language:** The more experience a social engineer has the better they are. A good social engineer can read and respond to their victim's body language and make connections with a person. They are able to recognize and adapt to emotions, and make their victim's feel comfortable. For example, if a social engineer has learned the body language of their victim, they can make a connection with a person from being compassionate. That person is more likely to feel obligated to help the SE out and do small favors for them such as letting them in a lab not knowing if that person has access or not (The official social engineering portal - security through education, 2015).

- **Gathering and Using Information:** The more information you have about your victim the more likely you are able to get what you want from them. Social engineers gather information from various resources whether it is traditional, non-traditional, or illegal. Traditional sources are public available sources that do not require illegal activity to obtain (Mickelberg, K., Pollard, N., & Schive, L. 2014). Examples of traditional sources are social networking sites such as LinkedIn, Facebook, or basic Google searches (The official social engineering portal - security through education, 2015). Non-traditional searches such as dumpster diving is legal and very common and often provide lots of information. Other methods to obtain information are by doing so illegally. Illegal ways to gather information are by gathering personal items such as security badges, uniforms, or smart phones from unlocked cars (The official social engineering portal - security through education, 2015). SE can also obtain information from malware, theft, and impersonating law enforcement or government agencies (Mickelberg, K., Pollard, N., & Schive, L. 2014).

Social engineering follows a set pattern or cycle of four steps that are easily recognizable to knowledgeable personnel when exploits commence. This cycle consists of information gathering, developing a relationship, exploitation, and execution. During the information gathering stage, a variety of techniques can be used by an aggressor to gather information about the target. These techniques include the following:

- Baiting - when an attacker leaves a malware-infected physical device, such as a USB flash drive or CD-ROM, in a place it will be found. The finder then picks up the device and loads it onto his or her computer, unintentionally installing the malware.

- Phishing - when a malicious party sends a fraudulent email disguised as a legitimate email, often purporting to be from a trusted source. The message is meant to trick the recipient into installing malware on their computer or device, or sharing personal or financial information.
- Spam – receiving unsolicited junk email with possible malware embedded.
- Spear phishing - like phishing, but tailored for a specific individual, group, or organization. In these cases, the attacker is trying to uncover confidential information specific to the receiving organization in order to obtain financial data or trade secrets (Rouse, 2018).

3. RAPID EXPANSION OF CYBERCRIME

Cybercrimes are any crimes that involve a network and a computer. The crimes can either be committed on the computer or the computer can be the target of the crime. Cybercrime is often made up of traditional crimes such as identity theft, fraud, cyberstalking, cyber bullying and child pornography (Allen, 2006).

According to the Pew Research Center's State of Cybercrime Survey (Pew Research Center, 2014), cybercrime ranked as the top national security threat, above terrorism, weapons of mass destruction and espionage (Mercer, n.d.). Cybercriminals have no preference in which businesses they choose to attack. The attacks range from small banks, to major defense contractors and even leading retailers. These criminals commit cybercrimes for a plethora of reasons. Some reasons are financial gain, curiosity, revenge, greed, lack of infrastructure, non-financial personal benefit, or excitement (Mickelberg, K., Pollard, N., & Schive, L. 2014). Crimes that are done for non-financial benefit like a jealous boyfriend hacking into a girlfriend's social media account or a teenager taking down a website just to prove that they can do it; can still have a serious impact or cause substantial property damage (Norton (2019). Most crimes committed for financial gain are committed outside of the Internet. Businessweek estimates that cybercrimes targeting online banking alone, pull in nearly 700 million dollars per year globally (Anah Bijik Hassan et. al. 2012). Having state of the art information technology devices are very important to help in proper monitoring. One of the reasons for the rise in cybercrime in Nigeria, is because Nigeria can't afford to keep up with the latest technology because of the current economic recession. The lack of a proper infrastructure creates an open avenue for these types of crimes to occur (Iozzio, 2008).

Cybercriminals work twice as hard to maintain an advantage against the security measures that businesses and government agencies implement; after all it's their job to do so. But not all cybercrimes occur from the outside. The Figure below taken from (US cybercrime: Rising risks, reduced readiness, 2018) shows the causes and consequences of cybercrimes committed by insiders. Social engineering made up 21% of the methods used to commit the cybercrimes. Cybercrimes can have a detrimental effect on an organization, which can damage a company's reputation as well as lose loyal customers. It can result in a loss of revenue, loss of confidential and propriety data as well as critical system disruption.

Figure 1. The causes and consequences of cybercrime committed by insiders

Most adverse consequences	Loss of confidential/proprietary data 11%	Reputational harm 11%	Critical system disruption 8%	Loss of current or future revenue 7%	Loss of customers 6%
Mechanisms used	Social engineering 21%	Laptops 18%	Remote access 17%	E-mail 17%	Copy data to mobile device 16%
Characteristics displayed	Violation of IT security policies 27%	Misuse of organization's resources 18%	Disruptive workplace behavior 10%	Formal reprimands/disciplinary action 8%	Poor performance reviews 7%
Reasons for committing cybercrime	Financial gain 16%	Curiosity 12%	Revenge 10%	Non-financial personal benefit 7%	Excitement 6%

* A current or former employee, service provider, authorized user of internal systems, or contractor

Hackers pride themselves on being able to hack a system, some would like to go down in history for being known to successfully perform the act, and then you have some that pride themselves on successfully doing so but never getting caught. According to the website (Iozzio, 2008), the best criminal hacker is the one that isn't caught-or even identified. Some of the unsolved cases are:

In February 1999, a small group of hackers gained control of the military's Ministry of Defense Skynet Satellite. These hackers disrupted a critical system and military communications, which could have resulted in something much more detrimental. The hackers were able to reprogram the control system before they were discovered. No arrest were ever made

In the CD Universe Credit Card Breach of 2000. The hacker Maxim demanded $100,000 from CDUniverse.com in exchange for destroying the 300,000 credit card numbers that he or she stole from the website. The result in this cybercrime ended up in the customer's personal information being stolen, the company's reputation being damaged, as well as a loss of customers. The case remains unsolved.

Although all cybercrimes are not always solved, the fact remains that cybercrimes are steadily on the rise. Statistics have shown that social engineering plays a major role in many insider cybercrimes resulting from employee vulnerabilities. These risks could be mitigated by implementing preventative measures.

4. THE ECONOMIC DIMENSION AND IMPACTS OF CYBERCRIMES

The average annual cost of cybercrime incurred per organization was totalled at $11.56 million, with a range bet2ween $1.3 million and $58 millions. This means, there is an increase of 26 percent, or $2.6 million in average cost in 2012. Organizations in the defense area, the financial services and energy and utilities sectors suffered the highest cybercrime losses. Thefts on Data caused major costs, 43 percent of the total external costs, business disruption or lost productivity accounts for 36% of external costs. While the data theft decreased by 2% in the last year, business disruption increased by 18%. Organizations experienced an average of 122 successful attacks per week, up from 102 attacks per week in 2012.

The average time it takes to resolve a cyber-attack was 32 days, with an average cost incurred during this period of $1,035,769, or $32,469 per day. This represents a 55 percent increase over the year 2011, which was estimated at an average cost of $591,780 for a 24-day period.

Denial-of-service, web-based attacks and insiders account for more than 55% of overall annual cybercrime costs per organization. Smaller organizations incur a significantly higher per-capita cost than larger organizations. Recovery and detection are the costliest internal activities (McAfee, 2014).

5. RECOMMENDED PREVENTATIVE MEASURES

The following are some measures that e-commerce businesses should adopt in order to secure their data, especially since they are more vulnerable to cyber thefts when compared to traditional brick and mortar businesses (Peters, Sara, 2015):

- **Choose a secure e-commerce platform.** Put your e-commerce site on a platform that uses a sophisticated object-oriented programming language.
- **Don't store sensitive data.** There is no reason to store thousands of records on your customers, especially credit card numbers, expiration dates and CVV2 (card verification value) codes.
- **Require strong passwords.** While it is the responsibility of the retailer to keep customer information safe on the back-end, you can help customers

help themselves by requiring a minimum number of characters and the use of symbols or numbers.

- **Set up system alerts for suspicious activity.** Set an alert notice for multiple and suspicious transactions coming through from the same IP address.
- **Layer your security.** One of the best ways to keep your business safe from cybercriminals is layering your security.
- **Provide security training to employees.** Employees need to know they should never email or text sensitive data or reveal private customer information in chat sessions as none of these communication methods is secure (Turban, E., Volonino, L., & Wood, G. (2020).

Hackers are stealing credit cards and other sensitive information from ecommerce sites. To protect (and reassure) your customers, it's imperative to know how to protect your e-business and your sensitive customer data (Schiff, Jennifer, L. 2013).

Social engineering is one of the largest gaps in a company's Information Technology Security plan, which has contributed to the rise in cybercrime. Having safeguards in place can help lower the risk associated with social engineering. One of the reasons that employees and companies fall victim to these cons, are because companies do not train their employees and promote awareness, companies do not have policies in place, and the network infrastructure is not solid.

- *Security Awareness*: Awareness training is a simple solution, yet the number one defense preventative measure. If people are aware of what social engineering attacks are, as well as the different tactics they are less likely to become a victim. Without the proper education people will not recognize a social engineer's trickery. Security awareness training should be an annual mandatory training for all employees to attend. It is important that the training is held annually to incorporate any new tactics that social engineers are using.
- *Policy*: Having a sound and well-written security policy in place is a key control that should be implemented. The policy sets the standard for the dos and the don'ts of the company. It should include, but not limited to: information labeling, how to handle email from unknown senders or unknown sites, not providing non-confidential or confidential information over the phone, via email or in person to suspicious sources, and an incident response strategy. The policy should give a clear direction to the employees of how to handle situations.
- *Security Architecture*: Having a solid and secure infrastructure in place provides detective controls to protect against cyber-attacks. A company should ensure that firewalls, Intrusion protection, intrusion detection, virus

protections, 2-factor authentication, etc. are implemented. An administrator should know how a network would respond in the event certain events happen.

- *Recovery Plan*: Because controls are not completely effective in preventing attacks a recovery plan should be implemented as a best practice. When attacks happen, they should be investigated and well documented to determine the cause as well as to assess the damage. In addition, the policies and security infrastructure should be reviewed and adjusted to prevent the attacks from recurring.

6. CONCLUSION

In conclusion, in spite of improvements in defense measures and the increased level of sensitization of cyber threats the cybercrimes ecosystem is able to implement more sophisticated cyber-attack tactics. The cybercrime industry is even getting quite immune and resilient in its capacity to adapt, quickly and successfully respond to countermeasures being put up by the police and crime fighters (McAfee, 2014).

Social engineering is not something new and it will be around for many centuries to come. As technology advances so will the tactics of cybercriminals. As long as humans exist, revenge, greed, coercion, and pride will exist and will continue to be factors in cybercrimes. Companies must continue taking a stance in minimizing cybercrimes due to social engineering. Enforcing awareness, implementing solid policies and securing infrastructures are just a start in taking a stand. Although, taking the appropriate countermeasures will help in preventing social engineering attacks, humans will always be a vulnerability and the weakest link of any network.

REFERENCES

Allen, M. (2006). *Social engineering. A means to violate a computer system.* Academic Press.

Currie, D. (2003). *Shedding some light on Voice Authentication.* SANS Institute. Retrieved from: https://www.sans.org/reading-room/whitepapers/authentication/shedding-light-voice-authentication-847

Goodchild, J. (2012, December 20). *Social engineering: the basics.* Retrieved November 2, 2015, from https://www.csoonline.com/article/2124681/security-awareness/social-engineering-the-basics.html

Hassan. (2012). Cybercrime in Nigeria: Causes, Effects and the Way Out. *ARPN Journal of Science and Technology, 2*(7). Retrieved from: http://www. ejournalofscience.org/archive/vol2no7/vol2no7_11.pdf

Heary, J. (n.d.). *Top 5 social engineering exploit techniques*. Retrieved November 2, 2015, from https://www.pcworld.com/article/182180

Iozzio, C. (2008, September 26). *The 10 most mysterious cyber crimes*. Retrieved November 2, 2015, from http://www.pcmag.com/article2/0,2817,2331225,00.asp

McAfee. (2014). *Net Losses: Estimating the Global Cost of Cybercrime Economic impact of cybercrime II*. Center for Strategic and International Studies.

Mercer, E. (n.d.). *Causes of cyber crime*. Retrieved November 2, 2015, from http:// science.opposingviews.com/causes-cyber-crime-1846.html

Mickelberg, K., Pollard, N., & Schive, L. (2014). *US cybercrime: rising risks, reduce readiness*. Retrieved November 2, 2015, from https://www.pwc.com/us/ en/increasing-it-effectiveness/publications/assets/2014-us-state-of-cybercrime.pdf

Norton. (n.d.). *The Definition of cybercrime*. Retrieved November 2, 2015, from https://us.norton.com/cybercrime-definition/promo

Peters, S. (2015 March 17) Information Week, *The Seven Best Social Engineering Attacks Ever*. https://www.darkreading.com/the-7-best-social-engineering-attacks-ever/d/d-id/1319411

Pew Research Center. (2020). *Cyber Attacks Likely to Increase*. Retrieved from: https://www.pewinternet.org/2014/10/29/cyber-attacks-likely-to-increase/

Reasons for the rise in cyber crime in Nigeria. (n.d.). Retrieved November 2, 2015, from https://martinslibrary.blogspot.com/2013/08/reasons-for-rise-in-cyber-crime-in.html

Rouse, M. (2015). *Social engineering*. Retrieved from https://searchsecurity. techtarget.com/definition/social-engineerring

Schiff, J. L. (2013 June 19). *15 Ways to Protect Your Ecommerce Site From Hacking and Fraud*. http://www.cio.com/article/2384809/e-commerce/15-ways-to-protect-your-ecommerce-site- from-hacking-and-fraud.html

The official social engineering portal - security through education. (2015). Retrieved November 2, 2015, from https://www.social-engineer.org/

Turban, E., Volonino, L., & Wood, G. (2020). *Information Technology For Management: Digital Strategies for Insight, Action, and Sustainable Performance* (10th ed.). John Wiley & Sons, Inc.

US cybercrime: Rising risks, reduced readiness. (2018). *US State of cybercrime Survey.* https://collabra.email/wp-content/uploads/2015/04/2014-us-state-of-cybercrime.pdf

Chapter 10
Essential Security Elements and Phases of Hacking Attacks

C. V. Anchugam
BCA Department, Vidyavahini First Grade College, Bengaluru, India

ABSTRACT

Cyber security provides protection against theft of data, protects computers from theft, minimizes computer freezing, provides privacy for users, and offers strict regulation. Firewalls can be difficult to configure correctly. Faultily configured firewalls may prohibit users from performing any behavior on the internet before the firewall is properly installed, and you will continue to upgrade the latest software to retain current protection. Cyber protection can be expensive for ordinary users. This is chapter helps to understand phases of attacks and types of attacks. Ethical hacking simulates a malicious attack without trying to cause damage. If you need to understand the countermeasures, first you need to understand the phases of an attack. It is necessary to comprehend the steps to counter an attack once it is detected and stop the attack before it reaches the next phase. In general, there are five phases that make up an attack such as reconnaissance, scanning, gaining access, maintaining access, covering tracks.

INTRODUCTION

Today an individual can receive and send any information may be video, or an email or only through the click of a button but did s/he ever ponder how safe this information transmitted to another individual strongly with no spillage of data? The proper response lies in cyber security. Today more than industry exchanges are done on the internet, so this area prerequisite high quality of security for direct

DOI: 10.4018/978-1-7998-6504-9.ch010

and best exchanges. Thus, cyber security has become a most recent issue. The extent of cyber security does not merely restrict to verifying the data in IT industry yet also to different fields like cyberspace and so forth. Improving cyber security and ensuring that necessary data systems are vital to each country's security and financial prosperity.

Cyber security has become a major concern over the last 10 year in the IT world. In the present world, everybody is facing a lot of problems with cybercrime. As hackers are hacking major sensitive information from government and some enterprise organizations the individuals are very much worried as cyber security assault can bring about everything from wholesale fraud, to blackmail big companies. They are many varieties of cyber-crimes emerging where everyone needs to be aware of the scams and they are different measures and tools which can be used for avoiding the cyber-crimes. Every organization wants to secure their confidential data from getting hacked.

Getting hacked is not just about losing the confidential data but losing the relationship with customers in the market The Internet is today's fastest growing infrastructure. In today's technical environment many new technologies are changing mankind. But due to these emerging technologies, we are unable to protect our private information in an efficient way, so the cyber-crimes are drastically increasing on daily basis.

Majority of the transactions both commercial and personal are done using the means online transaction, so it is important to have an expertise who require a high quality of security maintaining a better transparency to everyone and having safer transactions. So cyber security is the latest issue. Advanced technologies like cloud services, mobiles, E-commerce, internet banking and many more they require a high standards and safer process of security. All the tools and technologies involved for these transactions hold the most sensitive and crucial user information. So providing the necessary security to them is very important. Improving the cyber security and safeguarding the sensitive data and infrastructures are important to every countries top priority security.

Most people don't really understand what hacking is about, much less how to go about it. It's something that we just watch movies or hear about on the news. Companies are now acknowledging the potential dangers of these attacks and thinking of preemptive solutions - one of them being ethical hacking.

Everyone among us has one time or another has come across some form of attack. It could be physical or emotional or of some other kind. The intent is to cause some sort of harm – though sometimes it turn into a blessing in disguise. However, cyber attacks always aim at causing harm. They can be varied in their nature of approach and type of harm they inflict, depending on the motive, but the purpose is certainly malicious.

All of you must have encountered a situation when some unwanted changes, like installing some software or change your search engine, are made to your system or seen unwanted advertisements popping up while surfing Internet. These are examples of cyber attacks. These can range from being minor nuisance, like occasional popups, to creating havoc, like formatting hard disk.

Whether an attack is targeted or un-targeted or the attacker is using commodity or bespoke tools, cyber attacks have a number of stages in common. Some of these will meet their goal whilst others may be blocked. An attack, particularly if it is carried out by a persistent adversary, may consist of repeated stages. The attacker probing your defenses for weaknesses that, if exploitable, will take them closer to their ultimate goal. Understanding these stages will help to better defend you. Conventional cyber attacks affect primarily the confidentiality, integrity, and availability of data and services in cyberspace.

INFORMATION SECURITY

Security is "the quality or state of being secure – to be free from danger (Merriam-Webster, n.d.)." in other words, it protects adversaries, harm, worms, and attacks, intentionally or otherwise – is the objection. The history of information security begins with computer security. The need for computer security i.e., the need to secure physical locations, hardware, and software from threats— arise during World War II when the first mainframes, developed to aid computations for communication code breaking, were put to use. Multiple levels of security were implemented to protect these mainframes and maintain the integrity of their data. Access to sensitive military locations, for example, was controlled by means of badges, keys, and the facial recognition of authorized personnel by security guards. The growing need to maintain national security eventually led to more complex and more technologically sophisticated computer security safeguards. During these early years, information security was a straightforward process composed predominantly of physical security and simple document classification schemes. The primary threats to security were physical theft of equipment, espionage against the products of the systems, and sabotage. One of the first documented security problems that fell outside these categories occurred in the early 1960s, when a systems administrator was working on an MOTD (Message Of The Day) (Notes, 2015) file, and another administrator was editing the password file. A software glitch mixed the two files, and the entire password file was printed on every output file.

WHAT IS SECURITY?

Security is "the quality or state of being secure to be free from danger". It means, protection against adversaries from those who would do harm, intentionally or otherwise is the objective. National security, for example, is a multilayered system that protects the sovereignty of a state, its assets, its resources, and its people. Achieving the appropriate level of security for an organization also requires a multifaceted system.

A successful organization should have the following multiple layers of security in place to protect its operations:

- Physical security, to protect physical items, objects, or areas from unauthorized access and misuse
- Personnel security, to protect the individual or group of individuals who are authorized to access the organization and its operations
- Operations security, to protect the details of a particular operation or series of activities
- Communications security, to protect communications media, technology, and content
- Network security, to protect networking components, connections, and contents
- Information security, to protect the confidentiality, integrity and availability of information assets, whether in storage, processing, or transmission. It is achieved via the application of policy, education, training and awareness, and technology.

The Committee on National Security Systems (CNSS) defines information security as the protection of information and its critical elements, including the systems and hardware that use, store, and transmit that information (National Security Telecommunications and Information Systems Security, 1994). Information security includes the broad areas of information security management, computer and data security, and network security. The CNSS model of information security evolved from a concept developed by the computer security industry called the C.I.A. triangle.

The C.I.A. triangle has been the industry standard for computer security since the development of the mainframe. It is based on the three characteristics of information that give it value to organizations: confidentiality, integrity, and availability. The security of these three characteristics of information is as important today as it has always been, but the C.I.A. triangle model no longer adequately addresses the constantly changing environment. The threats to the confidentiality, integrity, and availability of information have evolved into a vast collection of events, including accidental or intentional damage, destruction, theft, unintended or unauthorized modification, or other misuse from human or nonhuman threats. This new environment of many constantly evolving threats has prompted the development of a more robust model that addresses the complexities of the current information security environment.

Information security is the protection of information and systems from unauthorized access, disclosure, modification, destruction or disruption.

MAIN PRINCIPLE OF INFORMATION SECURITY

There are three main principle of Information Security commonly known as CIA – Confidentiality, Integrity, and Availability.

Figure 1.

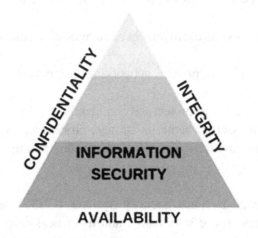

A. Confidentiality

Confidentiality is the protection of information which allows authorized users to access sensitive data. It involves any information that is sensitive and should only be shared with a limited number of people. The following types of information that is considered as confidential:

- Name, date of birth, age and address
- Contact information
- Bank account details

- Professional information
- Email account details
- Social Media Profile
- Medial record and Family information

B. Integrity

Integrity means maintaining the consistency, accuracy, and completeness of information. It involves keeping the information from being altered or changed and ensures that data cannot be altered by unauthorized people.

C. Availability

Availability ensures that information and resources are accessible for authorized users. If an attacker is not able to compromise the first two principles then they may try to execute denial of service (DoS) attack. This attack would bring down the web server and making the website unavailable to legitimate users due to lack of availability.

CYBER SECURITY

"Cybersecurity is primarily about people, processes, and technologies working together to encompass the full range of threat reduction, vulnerability reduction, deterrence, international engagement, incident response, resiliency, and recovery policies and activities, including computer network operations, information assurance, law enforcement, etc." (Javat Point, n.d.a)

Cybersecurity is the protection of Internet-connected systems, including hardware, software, and data from cyber attacks. It is made up of two words one is cyber and other is security. Cyber is related to the technology which contains systems, network and programs or data. Whereas security related to the protection which includes systems security, network security and application and information security. It is the body of technologies, processes, and practices designed to protect networks, devices, programs, and data from attack, theft, damage, modification or unauthorized access. It may also be referred to as information technology security.

Define cybersecurity as the set of principles and practices designed to protect our computing resources and online information against threats. Due to the heavy dependency on computers in a modern industry that store and transmit an abundance of confidential and essential information about the people, cybersecurity is a critical function and needed insurance of many businesses.

Why Is Cybersecurity Important?

We live in a digital era which understands that our private information is more vulnerable than ever before. We all live in a world which is networked together, from internet banking to government infrastructure, where data is stored on computers and other devices. A portion of that data can be sensitive information, whether that be intellectual property, financial data, personal information, or other types of data for which unauthorized access or exposure could have negative consequences.

Cyber-attack is now an international concern and has given many concerns that hacks and other security attacks could endanger the global economy. Organizations transmit sensitive data across networks and to other devices in the course of doing businesses, and cybersecurity describes to protect that information and the systems used to process or store it.

As the volume of cyber-attacks grows, companies and organizations, especially those that deal information related to national security, health, or financial records, need to take steps to protect their sensitive business and personal information.

CYBER SECURITY PRINCIPLES

The UK internet industry and Government (Javat Point, n.d.b) recognized the need to develop a series of Guiding Principles for improving the online security of the ISPs' customers and limit the rise in cyber-attacks. Cybersecurity for these purposes encompasses the protection of essential information, processes, and systems, connected or stored online, with a broad view across the people, technical, and physical domains. These Principles recognize that the ISPs (and other service providers), internet users, and UK Government all have a role in minimizing and mitigating the cyber threats inherent in using the internet.

These Guiding Principles have been developed to respond to this challenge by providing a consistent approach to help, inform, educate, and protect ISPs' (Internet Service Provider's) customers from online crimes. These Guiding Principles are inspirational, developed and delivered as a partnership between Government and ISPs. They recognize that ISPs have different sets of customers, offer different levels of support and services to protect those customers from cyber threats.

Key Elements of Cyber Security

Cyber security is the process and preventative action of protecting computer systems from malicious attacks or unauthorized access. The elements of cyber security are very important for every organization to protect their sensitive business information.

There are six essential key elements of cyber security such as application security, information security, network security, disaster recovery plan, operational and end user security which are as follows:

1. Application security
2. Information Security
3. Network Security
4. Disaster Recovery Planning
5. Operational Security
6. End User Education

1. Application Security

Application security is the first key elements of cyber security which adding security features within applications during development period to prevent from cyber attacks. It protects websites and web based application from different types of cyber security threats which exploit vulnerabilities in a source code. The application threats or vulnerabilities can be SQL injection, Denial of service attacks (DoS), data encryption, data breaches or other types of threats. The most common categories of application threats related to software or application are as follows:

1. Input validation
2. Authorization
3. Session management
4. Parameter tampering
5. Encryption

Different types of application security tools such as firewalls, antivirus software, encryption technique and Web Application Firewall (WAF) can help your application to prevent from cyber-attacks and unauthorized access.

2. Information Security

Information security (IS) or Info Sec refers to the process and methodology to preventing unauthorized access, use, disclosure, disruption, modification, or destruction of information. The information can be can be anything like your personal details, login credentials, network details or your profile on social media, mobile phone etc.

3. Network Security

Network security is another element of IT security which process of preventing and protecting against unauthorized access into computer networks. It is a set of rules and configurations to prevent and monitor unauthorized access, misuse, modification of a computer network and resources. It includes both hardware and software technologies. There are many methods to improve network security and the most common network security components are as follows:

1. Antivirus Software
2. Email Security
3. Firewalls
4. Virtual Private Network (VPN)
5. Web Security
6. Wireless Security
7. Endpoint Security
8. Network Access Control (NAC)

There are varieties of software and hardware tools to protect your computer network. Such as firewall, a network security tool which keep track of network traffic and what's happening on your networks. Following various example firewalls such as network firewalls cyber roam firewalls, web application firewalls, unified threat management, cloud firewalls.

4. Disaster Recovery Planning

A Disaster Recovery Plan (DRP) (CIO Wiki, n.d.) is a business continuity plan and managed procedures that describe how work can be resumed quickly and effectively after a disaster. A disaster recovery strategy should start at the business level and determine which applications are most important to running the organization activities. When disaster recovery strategies have been developed and approved, then organization can be translated into disaster recovery plans.

Steps of Disaster Recovery Planning

There are 12 steps to help you to prepare a disaster recovery plan which are as follows:

1. Define scope of the organization assets
2. Identifying the possible threats and vulnerabilities
3. Ensure Data Protection

4. Create a Disaster Recovery Team
5. Provide training to team members
6. Establish team member's accountability
7. Create a data recovery plan
8. Test your data recovery plan
9. Review regularly
10. Take back up regularly
11. Update and Revise Your Plan and
12. Possible to implement Cloud Backup

Types of Disaster Recovery Plans

There are about four types of disaster recovery plans and according to your business nature you can pick which plan best suits your needs.

1. Data Center Disaster Recovery
2. Cloud-Based Disaster Recovery
3. Virtualization Disaster Recovery
4. Disaster Recovery as a Service

5. Operational Security

Operational security (OPSEC) is an analytical and risk management process that identifies the organization's critical information and developing a protection mechanism to ensure the security of sensitive information. It is also known as procedural security which encourages manager to view operations in order to protect sensitive information.

Steps of Operational Security

To develop an effective operations security program, the organization's OPSEC officer's first find out and define the possible threats and then they will take necessary action. There are five steps to process the operational security program, which are as follows:

1. Define the organization sensitive information
2. Identify the categories of threats
3. Analyze security holes and vulnerabilities
4. Assessment of Risks
5. Implementation of appropriate countermeasures

6. End User Education

End user education is most important element of Computer security. End users are becoming the largest security risk in any organization because it can happen anytime. However, end user has no fault of their own, and mostly due to a lack of awareness and business security policies, procedures and protocols. There are many reasons, that a threat can be created. The end user threats can be created according to following ways are using of social media, text messaging, Apps download, use of Email, password creation and usages, etc.,

THE FIVE PILLARS OF CYBER SECURITY READINESS

1. Education and Awareness

First and foremost, it's essential that cybersecurity forms part of the conversation in every organization, from the lunch room to the boardroom. Only through keeping cybersecurity front of mind can it form part of the decision-making process, infrastructure investment, and regulatory and governance requirements. Additionally, as people can themselves be an attack vector through social engineering, everyone within an organization ultimately shares responsibility in ensuring best practice cybersecurity processes are carried out. This requires staff education with regular updates to material as new threats arise. In fact, parallels have been drawn between cybersecurity and healthcare – everyone needs some form of cybersecurity education. Finally, the employment of qualified cybersecurity professionals or certified training for key staff both in IT and management should form part of any cybersecurity readiness.

2. Planning and Preparation

A cybersecurity incident isn't an 'if' but a 'when', and to that end, preparation is essential. This can include management systems, best practice policies, IT auditing, and dedicated staff responsible for cybersecurity operations. Good cybersecurity readiness encompasses an understanding of risks and threats to assets and information relevant to the organization and its people, monitoring and detecting cybersecurity threats regularly, protecting critical systems and information, ensuring the organization meets all relevant standards compliance, has incident response plans in place in the event of a breach, and clear business continuity plans to minimize any loss. Typically, many of the above responsibilities belong to the CISO (Chief Information Security Officer) or equivalent, though other stakeholders such as senior leadership, legal and communications staff, and public relations may also need to have preparations in the event of an incident.

3. Detection and Recovery

When a breach happens, the quicker it is detected and responded to, the greater the chance of minimizing loss – be it financial, reputational, or otherwise. How quickly can your organization identify and respond to the theft of data or the disabling of key services? How fast can affected servers or workstations be quarantined for forensic analysis? How quickly and easily can lost or corrupted data be restored? What is the incident response plan and who are the stakeholders that need to be notified immediately? Importantly, the preservation and analysis of logs that can help identify how the breach happened, and thus how it can be closed, is part of the recovery process. It's not enough just to close the hole; an understanding of how the breach occurred can lead to preventing other, similar, breaches.

4. Sharing and Collaboration

As we've covered in this guide, collaboration is essential to mitigating current and future risks. Sharing the results of your breach analysis with government and industry can help stop a known attack vector hitting other organizations. In turn, your company may be able to prevent an exploit by learning from a breach that another organization shared. Also consider joining or providing information to an ISAC (Information Sharing and Analysis Centers, www.nationalisacs.org) (Kumar, 2019) if there is an equivalent for your industry. In some cases, your organization may be bound by legislative requirements to report an incident. At a minimum, a breach should be reported to government or organizations such as AusCERT and the Australian Centre for Cyber Security.

5. Ethics and Certification

It may initially seem a less practical pillar, but the difference between a 'white hat' hacker and 'black hat' hacker is mindset. In any company or organization, ethics plays a role and should be of particular concern when it comes to cybersecurity. While some sectors, such as defence, will have their own means to vet credentials, for an industry as diverse and skilled as ICT it helps if professionals can demonstrate adherence to a code of ethics through membership of a professional institution. Many professional organizations hold their members to standards that ensure the reputation and respectability of a profession is preserved. ACS, for example, has a code of ethics all Certified Professionals must abide by, in addition to other requirements such as demonstrating continued education and personal development in their chosen professional field of expertise.

ETHICAL HACKING

What Is Ethical Hacking?

Hacking (Ellis, n.d.) is the process of finding vulnerabilities in a system and using these found vulnerabilities to gain unauthorized access into the system to perform malicious activities ranging from deleting system files to stealing sensitive information. Hacking is illegal and can lead to extreme consequences if you are caught in the act. People have been sentenced to years of imprisonment because of hacking.

Nonetheless, hacking can be legal if done with permission. Computer experts are often hired by companies to hack into their system to find vulnerabilities and weak endpoints so that they can be fixed. This is done as a precautionary measure against legitimate hackers who have malicious intent. Such people, who hack into a system with permission, without any malicious intent, are known as ethical hackers and the process is known as ethical hacking.

Ethical Hackers check for key vulnerabilities includes but is not limited to:

- Injection attacks
- Changes in security settings
- Exposure of sensitive data
- Breach in authentication protocols
- Components used in the system or network that may be used as access points

Roles and Responsibilities of an Ethical Hacker

Ethical Hackers must follow certain guidelines in order to perform hacking legally. A good hacker knows his or her responsibility and adheres to all of the ethical guidelines. Here are the most important rules of Ethical Hacking:

- An ethical hacker must seek authorization from the organization that owns the system. Hackers should obtain complete approval before performing any security assessment on the system or network.
- Determine the scope of their assessment and make known their plan to the organization.
- Report any security breaches and vulnerabilities found in the system or network.

- Keep their discoveries confidential. As their purpose is to secure the system or network, ethical hackers should agree to and respect their non-disclosure agreement.
- Erase all traces of the hack after checking the system for any vulnerability. It prevents malicious hackers from entering the system through the identified loopholes.

Benefits of Ethical Hacking

Learning ethical hacking involves studying the mindset and techniques of black hat hackers and testers to learn how to identify and correct vulnerabilities within networks. Studying ethical hacking can be applied by security pros across industries and in a multitude of sectors. This sphere includes network defender, risk management, and quality assurance tester.

However, the most obvious benefit of learning ethical hacking is its potential to inform and improve and defend corporate networks. The primary threat to any organization's security is a hacker: learning, understanding, and implementing how hackers operate can help network defenders prioritize potential risks and learn how to remediate them best. Additionally, getting an ethical hacking training or certifications can benefit those who are seeking a new role in the security realm or those wanting to demonstrate skills and quality to their organization.

Skills Required Becoming an Ethical Hacker

An ethical hacker should have in-depth knowledge about all the systems, networks, program codes, security measures, etc. to perform hacking efficiently. Some of these skills include:

- Knowledge of programming - It is required for security professionals working in the field of application security and Software Development Life Cycle (SDLC).
- Scripting knowledge - This is required for professionals dealing with network-based attacks and host-based attacks.
- Networking skills - This skill is important because threats mostly originate from networks. You should know about all of the devices present in the network, how they are connected, and how to identify if they are compromised.
- Understanding of databases - Attacks is mostly targeted at databases. Knowledge of database management systems such as SQL will help you to effectively inspect operations carried out in databases.
- Knowledge of multiple platforms like Windows, Linux, Unix, etc.

- The ability to work with different hacking tools available in the market.
- Knowledge of search engines and servers.

5 Phases of Hacking

How the daily hacks are performed and to protect you from such incidents atleast take some precautions.

1. Reconnaissance

This is the first phase where the Hacker tries to collect information about the target. It may include Identifying the Target, finding out the target's IP Address Range, Network, DNS records, etc. It is also called as Footprinting and information gathering Phase. This is the preparatory phase where we collect as much information as possible about the target. We usually collect information about three groups,

1. Network
2. Host
3. People involved

There are two types of Footprinting:

1. **Active:** Directly interacting with the target to gather information about the target. Eg Using Nmap tool to scan the target
2. **Passive:** Trying to collect the information about the target without directly accessing the target. This involves collecting information from social media, public websites etc.

Let's assume that an attacker is about to hack a websites' contacts.He may do so by: using a search engine like maltego, researching the target say a website (checking links, jobs, job titles, email, news, etc.), or a tool like HTTPTrack to download the entire website for later enumeration, the hacker is able to determine the following: Staff names, positions, and email addresses.

2. Scanning

This phase includes usage of tools like dialers, port scanners, network mappers, sweepers, and vulnerability scanners to scan data. Hackers are now probably seeking any information that can help them perpetrate attack such as computer names, IP addresses, and user accounts. Now that the hacker has some basic information;

the hacker now moves to the next phase and begins to test the network for other avenues of attacks. The hacker decides to use a couple methods for this end to help map the network (i.e. Kali Linux, Maltego and find an email to contact to see what email server is being used). The hacker looks for an automated email if possible or based on the information gathered he may decide to email HR with an inquiry about a job posting.

Figure 2. Scanning example

```
root@kali:~# nmap -sT 192.168.89.191 -p25-150

Starting Nmap 6.40 ( http://nmap.org ) at 2014-09-05 16:19 EDT
mass_dns: warning: Unable to determine any DNS servers. Reverse DNS is disabled.
Try using --system-dns or specify valid servers with --dns-servers
Nmap scan report for 192.168.89.191
Host is up (0.0017s latency).
Not shown: 120 closed ports
PORT     STATE SERVICE
25/tcp   open  smtp
53/tcp   open  domain
80/tcp   open  http
110/tcp  open  pop3
135/tcp  open  msrpc
139/tcp  open  netbios-ssn
MAC Address: 00:0C:29:18:6B:DB (VMware)

Nmap done: 1 IP address (1 host up) scanned in 0.18 seconds
root@kali:~#
```

Three types of scanning are involved:

- **Port scanning:** This phase involves scanning the target for the information like open ports, Live systems, various services running on the host.
- **Vulnerability Scanning:** Checking the target for weaknesses or vulnerabilities which can be exploited. Usually done with help of automated tools
- **Network Mapping:** Finding the topology of network, routers, firewalls servers if any, and host information and drawing a network diagram with the available information. This map may serve as a valuable piece of information throughout the hacking process.

3. Gaining Access

In this phase, hacker designs the blueprint of the network of the target with the help of data collected during Phase 1 and Phase 2. The hacker has finished enumerating and scanning the network and now decides that they have a some options to gain access to the network. Where an attacker breaks into the system/network using various tools or methods. After entering into a system, he has to increase his privilege to administrator level so he can install an application he needs or modify data or hide data.

For example, Phishing Attack: The hacker decides to play it safe and use a simple phishing attack to gain access. The hacker decides to infiltrate from the IT department. They see that there have been some recent hires and they are likely not up to speed on the procedures yet. A phishing email will be sent using the CTO's actual email address using a program and sent out to the techs. The email contains a phishing website that will collect their login and passwords. Using any number of options (phone app, website email spoofing, Zmail, etc) the hacker sends a email asking the users to login to a new Google portal with their credentials. They already have the Social Engineering Toolkit running and have sent an email with the server address to the users masking it with a bitly or tinyurl (Smurf, 2015).

Other options include creating a reverse TCP/IP shell in a PDF using Metasploit (may be caught by spam filter). Looking at the event calendar they can set up a Evil Twin router and try to Man in the Middle attack users to gain access. A variant of Denial of Service attack, stack based buffer overflows, and session hijacking may also prove to be great.

4. Maintaining Access

Figure 3. Maintaining access example

Once a hacker has gained access, they want to keep that access for future exploitation and attacks. Once the hacker owns the system, they can use it as a base to launch additional attacks. In this case, the owned system is sometimes referred to as a zombie system. Now that the hacker has multiple e-mail accounts, the hacker begins to test the accounts on the domain. The hacker from this point creates a new administrator account for themselves based on the naming structure and try and blend in. As a precaution, the hacker begins to look for and identify accounts that have not been used for a long time. The hacker assumes that these accounts are likely either forgotten or not used so they change the password and elevate privileges to an administrator as a secondary account in order to maintain access to the network. The hacker may also send out emails to other users with an exploited file such as a PDF with a reverse shell in order to extend their possible access. No overt exploitation or attacks will occur at this time. If there is no evidence of detection, a waiting game is played letting the victim think that nothing was disturbed. With access to an IT account the hacker begins to make copies of all emails, appointments, contacts, instant messages, and files to be sorted through and used later.

5. Clearing Tracks (So No One Can Reach Them)

Prior to the attack, the attacker would change their MAC address and run the attacking machine through at least one VPN to help cover their identity. They will not deliver a direct attack or any scanning technique that would be deemed "noisy"(Smurf, 2015). Once access is gained and privileges have been escalated, the hacker seeks to cover their tracks. This includes clearing out Sent emails, clearing server logs, temp files, etc. The hacker will also look for indications of the email provider alerting the user or possible unauthorized logins under their account.

Protect Yourself: What and What Not to Do?

- Do not post information on social media that can be related to challenge questions
- Use passwords that cannot be broken by brute force or guessing.
- Consider 2 factor authentications when possible.
- Be careful of password requests emails. Services like Heroku, Gmail and others will not request to type in passwords for additional promotion or service.
- Verify source of contact.
- Before clicking a link, investigate it.
- Always scan a file and never click on batch files.
- Always see the background services that are running in your device and never rely on others' device.
- Be sure to have a antivirus installed and set root passwords for installation.
- Log out of sessions and clean the cache.

COMMON TYPES OF CYBER ATTACKS

A cyber attack is any type of offensive action that targets computer information systems, infrastructures, computer networks or personal computer devices, using various methods to steal, alter or destroy data or information systems. Most common cyber attack types are:

1. Denial-of-service (DoS) and distributed denial-of-service (DDoS) attacks
2. Man-in-the-middle (MitM) attack
3. Phishing and spear phishing attacks
4. Drive-by attack
5. Password attack
6. SQL injection attack
7. Cross-site scripting (XSS) attack
8. Eavesdropping attack
9. Birthday attack
10. Malware attack

1. Denial-of-service (DoS) and Distributed Denial-Of-Service (DDoS) Attacks

A denial-of-service attack overwhelms a system's resources so that it cannot respond to service requests. A DDoS attack is also an attack on system's resources, but it is launched from a large number of other host machines that are infected by malicious software controlled by the attacker.

Unlike attacks that are designed to enable the attacker to gain or increase access, denial-of-service doesn't provide direct benefits for attackers. For some of them, it's enough to have the satisfaction of service denial. However, if the attacked resource belongs to a business competitor, then the benefit to the attacker may be real enough. Another purpose of a DoS attack can be to take a system offline so that a different kind of attack can be launched. There are different types of DoS and DDoS attacks; the most common are TCP SYN flood attack, teardrop attack, smurf attack, ping-of-death attack and botnets.

TCP SYN Flood Attack

In this attack, an attacker exploits the use of the buffer space during a Transmission Control Protocol (TCP) session initialization handshake. The attacker's device floods the target system's small in-process queue with connection requests, but it does not respond when the target system replies to those requests. This causes the target system to time out while waiting for the response from the attacker's device, which makes the system crash or become unusable when the connection queue fills up. There are a few countermeasures to a TCP SYN flood attack:

- Place servers behind a firewall configured to stop inbound SYN packets.
- Increase the size of the connection queue and decrease the timeout on open connections.

Teardrop Attack

This attack causes the length and fragmentation offset fields in sequential Internet Protocol (IP) packets to overlap one another on the attacked host; the attacked system attempts to reconstruct packets during the process but fails. The target system then becomes confused and crashes. If users don't have patches to protect against this DoS attack, disable SMBv2 and block ports 139 and 445.

Smurf Attack

This attack involves using IP spoofing and the ICMP to saturate a target network with traffic. This attack method uses ICMP echo requests targeted at broadcast IP addresses. These ICMP requests originate from a spoofed "victim" address. For instance, if the intended victim address is 10.0.0.10, the attacker would spoof an ICMP echo request from 10.0.0.10 to the broadcast address 10.255.255.255. This request would go to all IPs in the range, with all the responses going back to 10.0.0.10, overwhelming the network. This process is repeatable, and can be automated to generate huge amounts of network congestion.

To protect your devices from this attack, you need to disable IP-directed broadcasts at the routers. This will prevent the ICMP echo broadcast request at the network devices. Another option would be to configure the end systems to keep them from responding to ICMP packets from broadcast addresses.

Ping of Death Attack

This type of attack uses IP packets to 'ping a target system with an IP size over the maximum of 65,535 bytes. IP packets of this size are not allowed, so attacker fragments the IP packet. Once the target system reassembles the packet, it can experience buffer overflows and other crashes. Ping of death attacks can be blocked by using a firewall that will check fragmented IP packets for maximum size.

Botnets

Botnets are the millions of systems infected with malware under hacker control in order to carry out DDoS attacks. These bots or zombie systems are used to carry out attacks against the target systems, often overwhelming the target system's bandwidth and processing capabilities. These DDoS attacks are difficult to trace because botnets are located in differing geographic locations. Botnets can be mitigated by:

- RFC3704 filtering, which will deny traffic from spoofed addresses and help ensure that traffic is traceable to its correct source network. For example, RFC3704 filtering will drop packets from bogon list addresses.
- Black hole filtering, which drops undesirable traffic before it enters a protected network. When a DDoS attack is detected, the BGP (Border Gateway Protocol) host should send routing updates to ISP routers so that they route all traffic heading to victim servers to a null0 interface at the next hop.

2. Man-in-the-Middle (MitM) Attack

A MitM attack occurs when a hacker inserts itself between the communications of a client and a server. Here are some common types of man-in-the-middle attacks:

Session Hijacking

In this type of MitM attack, an attacker hijacks a session between a trusted client and network server. The attacking computer substitutes its IP address for the trusted client while the server continues the session, believing it is communicating with the client. For instance, the attack might unfold like this:

1. A client connects to a server.
2. The attacker's computer gains control of the client.
3. The attacker's computer disconnects the client from the server.
4. The attacker's computer replaces the client's IP address with its own IP address andspoofs the client's sequence numbers.
5. The attacker's computer continues dialog with the server and the server believes it is still communicating with the client.

Figure 4. MiTM attack Example

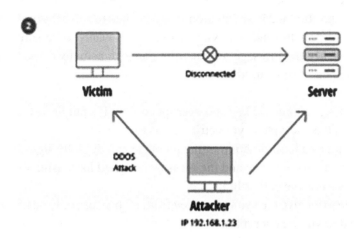

IP Spoofing

IP spoofing is used by an attacker to convince a system that it is communicating with a known, trusted entity and provide the attacker with access to the system. The attacker sends a packet with the IP source address of a known, trusted host instead of its own IP source address to a target host. The target host might accept the packet and act upon it.

Replay

A replay attack occurs when an attacker intercepts and saves old messages and then tries to send them later, impersonating one of the participants. This type can be easily countered with session timestamps or nonce (a random number or a string that changes with time). Currently, there is no single technology or configuration to prevent all MitM attacks (Hero, n.d.). Generally, encryption and digital certificates provide an effective safeguard against MitM attacks, assuring both the confidentiality and integrity of communications. But a man-in-the-middle attack can be injected into the middle of communications in such a way that encryption will not help — for example, attacker "A" intercepts public key of person "P" and substitute it with his own public key. Then, anyone wanting to send an encrypted message to P using P's public key is unknowingly using A's public key. Therefore, A can read the message intended for P and then send the message to P, encrypted in P's real public key, and P will never notice that the message was compromised. In addition, A could also modify the message before resending it to P. As you can see, P is using encryption and thinks that his information is protected but it is not, because of the MitM attack.

So, how can you make sure that P's public key belongs to P and not to A? Certificate authorities and hash functions were created to solve this problem. When person 2 (P2) wants to send a message to P, and P wants to be sure that A will not read or modify the message and that the message actually came from P2, the following method must be used:

1. P2 creates a symmetric key and encrypts it with P's public key.
2. P2 sends the encrypted symmetric key to P.
3. P2 computes a hash function of the message and digitally signs it.
4. P2 encrypts his message and the message's signed hash using the symmetric key and sends the entire thing to P.
5. P is able to receive the symmetric key from P2 because only he has the private key to decrypt the encryption.
6. P, and only P, can decrypt the symmetrically encrypted message and signed hash because he has the symmetric key.
7. He is able to verify that the message has not been altered because he can compute the hash of received message and compare it with digitally signed one.
8. P is also able to prove to himself that P2 was the sender because only P2 can sign the hash so that it is verified with P2 public key.

3. Phishing and Spear Phishing Attacks

Phishing attack is the practice of sending emails that appear to be from trusted sources with the goal of gaining personal information or influencing users to do something. It combines social engineering and technical trickery. It could involve an attachment to an email that loads malware onto your computer. It could also be a link to an illegitimate website that can trick you into downloading malware or handing over your personal information.

Spear phishing is a very targeted type of phishing activity. Attackers take the time to conduct research into targets and create messages that are personal and relevant. Because of this, spear phishing can be very hard to identify and even harder to defend against. One of the simplest ways that a hacker can conduct a spear phishing attack is email spoofing, which is when the information in the "From" section of the email is falsified, making it appear as if it is coming from someone you know, such as your management or your partner company. Another technique that scammers use to add credibility to their story is website cloning — they copy legitimate websites to fool you into entering personally identifiable information (PII) or login credentials.

To reduce the risk of being phished, you can use these techniques:

- **Critical thinking** — Do not accept that an email is the real deal just because you're busy or stressed or you have 150 other unread messages in your inbox. Stop for a minute and analyze the email.
- **Hovering over the links** — Move your mouse over the link, but do not click it! Just let your mouse cursor h over over the link and see where would actually take you. Apply critical thinking to decipher the URL.
- **Analyzing email headers** — Email headers define how an email got to your address. The "Reply-to" and "Return-Path" parameters should lead to the same domain as is stated in the email.
- **Sandboxing** — You can test email content in a sandbox environment, logging activity from opening the attachment or clicking the links inside the email.

4. Drive-by Attack

Drive-by download attacks are a common method of spreading malware. Hackers look for insecure websites and plant a malicious script into HTTP or PHP code on one of the pages. This script might install malware directly onto the computer of someone who visits the site, or it might re-direct the victim to a site controlled by the hackers. Drive-by downloads can happen when visiting a website or viewing an email message or a pop-up window. Unlike many other types of cyber security attacks, a drive-by doesn't rely on a user to do anything to actively enable the attack — you don't have to click a download button or open a malicious email attachment to become infected. A drive-by download can take advantage of an app, operating system or web browser that contains security flaws due to unsuccessful updates or lack of updates.

To protect yourself from drive-by attacks, you need to keep your browsers and operating systems up to date and avoid websites that might contain malicious code. Stick to the sites you normally use — although keep in mind that evens these sites can be hacked. Don't keep too many unnecessary programs and apps on your device. The more plug-ins you have, the more vulnerability there are that can be exploited by drive-by attacks.

5. Password Attack

Because passwords are the most commonly used mechanism to authenticate users to an information system, obtaining passwords is a common and effective attack approach. Access to a person's password can be obtained by looking around the person's desk, ''sniffing'' the connection to the network to acquire unencrypted passwords, using social engineering, gaining access to a password database or outright guessing. The last approach can be done in either a random or systematic manner:

- **Brute-force** password guessing means using a random approach by trying different passwords and hoping that one work some logic can be applied by trying passwords related to the person's name, job title, hobbies or similar items.
- In a **dictionary attack,** a dictionary of common passwords is used to attempt to gain access to a user's computer and network. One approach is to copy an encrypted file that contains the passwords, apply the same encryption to a dictionary of commonly used passwords, and compare the results.

In order to protect yourself from dictionary or brute-force attacks, you need to implement an account lockout policy that will lock the account after a few invalid password attempts. You can follow these account lockout best practices in order to set it up correctly .

6. SQL Injection Attack

SQL injection has become a common issue with database-driven websites. It occurs when a malefactor executes a SQL query to the database via the input data from the client to server. SQL commands are inserted into data-plane input (for example, instead of the login or password) in order to run predefined SQL commands. A successful SQL injection exploit can read sensitive data from the database, modify (insert, update or delete) database data, execute administration operations (such as shutdown) on the database, recover the content of a given file, and, in some cases, issue commands to the operating system.

For example, a web form on a website might request a user's account name and then send it to the database in order to pull up the associated account information using dynamic SQL like this:

```
"SELECT * FROM users WHERE account = '" +
userProvidedAccountNumber +"';"
```

While this works for users who are properly entering their account number, it leaves a hole for attackers. For example, if someone decided to provide an account number of *" ' or '1' = '1' "*, that would result in a query string of:

```
"SELECT * FROM users WHERE account = '' or '1' = '1';"
```

Because *'1' = '1'* always evaluates to TRUE, the database will return the data for all users instead of just a single user.

The vulnerability to this type of cyber security attack depends on the fact that SQL makes no real distinction between the control and data planes. Therefore, SQL injections work mostly if a website uses dynamic SQL. Additionally, SQL injection is very common with PHP and ASP applications due to the prevalence of older functional interfaces. J2EE and ASP.NET applications are less likely to have easily exploited SQL injections because of the nature of the programmatic interfaces available.

In order to protect yourself from a SQL injection attacks, apply least0privilege model of permissions in your databases. Stick to stored procedures (make sure that these procedures don't include any dynamic SQL) and prepared statements (parameterized queries). The code that is executed against the database must be strong enough to prevent injection attacks. In addition, validate input data against a white list at the application level.

7. Cross-site Scripting (XSS) Attack

XSS attacks use third-party web resources to run scripts in the victim's web browser or scriptable application. Specifically, the attacker injects a payload with malicious JavaScript into a website's database. When the victim requests a page from the website, the website transmits the page, with the attacker's payload as part of the HTML body, to the victim's browser, which executes the malicious script. For example, it might send the victim's cookie to the attacker's server, and the attacker can extract it and use it for session hijacking. The most dangerous consequences occur when XSS is used to exploit additional vulnerabilities. These vulnerabilities can enable an attacker to not only steal cookies, but also log key strokes, capture screenshots, discover and collect network information, and remotely access and control the victim's machine.

While XSS can be taken advantage of within VBScript, ActiveX and flash, the most widely abused is JavaScript — primarily because JavaScript is supported widely on the web.

To defend against XSS attacks, developers can sanitize data input by users in an HTTP request before reflecting it back. Make sure all data is validated, filtered or escaped before echoing anything back to the user, such as the values of query parameters during searches. Convert special characters such as ?, &, /, <, > and spaces to their respective HTML or URL encoded equivalents. Give users the option to disable client-side scripts.

Figure 5. XSS attack

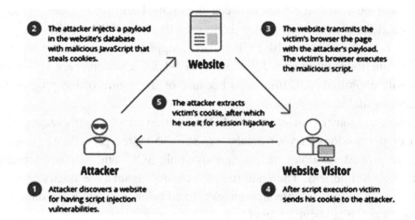

8. Eavesdropping Attack

Eavesdropping attacks occur through the interception of network traffic. By eavesdropping, an attacker can obtain passwords, credit card numbers and other confidential information that a user might be sending over the network. Eavesdropping can be passive or active:

- **Passive eavesdropping** — A hacker detects the information by listening to the message transmission in the network.
- **Active eavesdropping** — A hacker actively grabs the information by disguising himself as friendly unit and by sending queries to transmitters. This is called probing, scanning or tampering.

Detecting passive eavesdropping attacks is often more important than spotting active ones, since active attacks requires the attacker to gain knowledge of the friendly units by conducting passive eavesdropping before. Data encryption is the best countermeasure for eavesdropping.

9. Birthday Attack

Birthday attacks are made against hash algorithms that are used to verify the integrity of a message, software or digital signature. A message processed by a hash function produces a message digest (MD) of fixed length, independent of the length of the input message; this MD uniquely characterizes the message. The birthday attack refers to the probability of finding two random messages that generate the same

MD when processed by a hash function. If an attacker calculates same MD for his message as the user has, he can safely replace the user's message with his, and the receiver will not be able to detect the replacement even if he compares MDs.

10. Malware Attack

Malicious software can be described as unwanted software that is installed in your system without your consent. It can attach itself to legitimate code and propagate; it can lurk in useful applications or replicate itself across the Internet. Here are some of the most common types of malware:

- **Macro Viruses** — These viruses infect applications such as Microsoft Word or Excel. Macro viruses attach to an application's initialization sequence. When the application is opened, the virus executes instructions before transferring control to the application. The virus replicates itself and attaches to other code in the computer system.

- **File infectors** — File infector viruses usually attach themselves to executable code, such as .exe files. The virus is installed when the code is loaded. Another version of a file infector associates itself with a file by creating a virus file with the same name, but an .exe extension. Therefore, when the file is opened, the virus code will execute.

- **System or boot-record infectors** — A boot-record virus attaches to the master boot record on hard disks. When the system is started, it will look at the boot sector and load the virus into memory, where it can propagate to other disks and computers.

- **Polymorphic viruses** — These viruses conceal themselves through varying cycles of encryption and decryption. The encrypted virus and an associated mutation engine are initially decrypted by a decryption program. The virus proceeds to infect an area of code. The mutation engine then develops a new decryption routine and the virus encrypts the mutation engine and a copy of the virus with an algorithm corresponding to the new decryption routine. The encrypted package of mutation engine and virus is attached to new code, and the process repeats. Such viruses are difficult to detect but have a high level of entropy because of the many modifications of their source code. Anti-virus software or free tools like Process Hacker can use this feature to detect them.

- **Stealth viruses** — Stealth viruses take over system functions to conceal themselves. They do this by compromising malware detection software so that the software will report an infected area as being uninfected. These viruses conceal any increase in the size of an infected file or changes to the file's date and time of last modification.

- **Trojans** — A Trojan or a Trojan horse is a program that hides in a useful program and usually has a malicious function. A major difference between viruses and Trojans is that Trojans do not self-replicate. In addition to launching attacks on a system, a Trojan can establish a back door that can be exploited by attackers. For example, a Trojan can be programmed to open a high-numbered port so the hacker can use it to listen and then perform an attack.

- **Logic bombs** — A logic bomb is a type of malicious software that is appended to an application and is triggered by a specific occurrence, such as a logical condition or a specific date and time.

- **Worms** — Worms differ from viruses in that they do not attach to a host file, but are self-contained programs that propagate across networks and computers. Worms are commonly spread through email attachments; opening the attachment activates the worm program. A typical worm exploit involves the worm sending a copy of itself to every contact in an infected computer's email address In addition to conducting malicious activities, a worm spreading across the internet and overloading email servers can result in denial-of-service attacks against nodes on the network.

- **Droppers** — A dropper is a program used to install viruses on computers. In many instances, the dropper is not infected with malicious code and, therefore might not be detected by virus-scanning software. A dropper can also connect to the internet and download updates to virus software that is resident on a compromised system.

- **Ransomware** — Ransomware is a type of malware that blocks access to the victim's data and threatens to publish or delete it unless a ransom is paid. While some simple computer ransomware can lock the system in a way that is not difficult for a knowledgeable person to reverse, more advanced malware uses a technique called cryptoviral extortion, which encrypts the victim's files in a way that makes them nearly impossible to recover without the decryption key.

- **Adware** — Adware is a software application used by companies for marketing purposes; advertising banners are displayed while any program is running. Adware can be automatically downloaded to your system while browsing any website and can be viewed through pop-up windows or through a bar that appears on the computer screen automatically.

- **Spyware** — Spyware is a type of program that is installed to collect information about users, their computers or their browsing habits. It tracks everything you do without your knowledge and sends the data to a remote user. It also can download and install other malicious programs from the internet. Spyware works like adware but is usually a separate program that is installed unknowingly when you install another freeware application.

REFERENCES

CIO Wiki. (n.d.). *Disaster Recovery Plan (DRP)*. Retrieved from: https://cio-wiki. org/wiki/Disaster_Recovery_Plan_(DRP)

Ellis. (n.d.). Ethical Hacking. In *Computer and Information Security Handbook* (pp. 475-481). doi:10.1016/B978-0-12-803843-7.00030-2

Gur, Bahtiyar, & Algoz. (2015). Security analysis of computer networks. In *Modeling Simulation of Computer Networks and Systems*. Elsevier.

Hero, C. (n.d.). *Man in the Middle Attack*. Retrieved from: https://www.coursehero. com/file/p3u2v5p/Man-in-the-middle-MitM-attack-A-MitM-attack-occurs-when-a-hacker-inserts-itself/

Javat Point. (n.d.a). *Cyber Security Introduction*. Retrieved from: https:// www.javatpoint.com/cyber-security-introduction#:~:text="Cybersecurity%20 is%20 primarily%20about%20people,including%20computer%20network%20 operations%2C%20information

Javat Point. (n.d.b). *Cyber Security Principles*. Retrieved from: https://www.javatpoint. com/cyber-security-principles

Kumar, A. (2019). *Cyber Security*. Retrieved from: https://www.linkedin.com/ pulse"/cyber-security-amar-kumar/

Merriam-Webster. (n.d.). Security. *Merriam-webster online*. Accessed 18 October 2018 from www.m-w.com/dictionary/security

National Security Telecommunications and Information Systems Security. (1994). *National Training Standard for Information Systems Security (Infosec) Professionals*. Author.

Notes, M. C. (2015). *Information Security – Evolution*. Retrieved from: https:// thisismyclassnotes.blogspot.com/2015/06/information-security-evolution.html

Smurf, R. (2015). *The 5 Phases of a Phishing Attack*. Retrieved from: https://www. cybrary.it/blog/0p3n/anatomy-of-the-hack/

Chapter 11
The Dynamics of Social Engineering and Cybercrime in the Digital Age

Nabie Y. Conteh
Southern University at New Orleans, USA

DeAngela "Dee" Sword
University of Maryland Global Campus, USA

ABSTRACT

Social engineering attacks have emerged to become one of the most problematic tactics used against businesses today. Social engineers employ both human-based and computer-based tactics to successfully compromise their targeted networks. This chapter will discuss the basics of social engineering and what it means today. It will explain some common attack methods like baiting, phishing, pretexting, quid pro quo, tailgating, and dumpster diving. It will then highlight the impact social engineering has had on the rise in cybercrime and why threat actors have grown more innovative. Finally, this chapter will discuss what multi-layer defense or defense in depth is and offer countermeasures that can be enforced to defend against social engineering attacks.

I. INTRODUCTION

Social engineering, also known as human hacking, is the art of tricking employees and consumers into disclosing their credentials and then using them to gain access to networks or accounts. It is a hacker's tricky use of deception or manipulation of

DOI: 10.4018/978-1-7998-6504-9.ch011

people's tendency to trust, be corporative, or simply follow their desire to explore and be curious. Sophisticated IT security systems cannot protect systems from hackers or defend against what seems to be authorized access. People are easily hacked, making them and their social media posts high-risk attack targets. It is often easy to get computer users to infect their corporate network or mobiles by luring them to spoof websites and or tricking them into clicking on harmful links and or downloading and installing malicious applications and or backdoors.

Around the year 1250 $_{B.C}$, the Trojan War between the people of Troy and the Greeks had begun. It was not until 10 years later when the Trojan horse was erected and left outside of the city of Troy. The Trojans accepted the horse as a peace offering and pulled the mysterious gift into the city. A small group of Greek warriors laid awake inside of the horse as the city of Troy erupted in celebration. Once the city grew quiet, the Greeks climbed out of the wooden horse to let the rest of the army into the city. The Greeks were able to siege the entire city putting an end to the Trojan War before anyone could be alerted (Peters, 2015). Nearly 3,000 years later similar tactics are being used to exploit weaknesses in human behavior to achieve personal gains. Cybercriminals are capitalizing on people's tendencies to be helpful, trustful, and/or lazy with intention of gaining access to desired information or controlled areas. (Thapar, n.d.). Over the span of 5 years, companies like RSA, Target, and Twitter have been victims of sophisticated social engineering attacks. Each company has spent or lost millions of dollars in effort to recuperate from such attacks. As the Digital War between Cybersecurity professionals and Cybercriminals wages on. It is now more advantageous for organizations to understand the various types of social engineering attacks, how social engineering has stimulated cybercrime and incorporate countermeasures to prevent social engineering attacks than it has ever been before.

II. SOCIAL ENGINEERING DEFINED

Social Engineering is a form of deception that hackers use to acquire sensitive information, access to unauthorized infrastructure and facilities. There are two main categories under which all social engineering attempts can be classified either technology based deception or human based deception (Thapar, n.d.). With technical tactics, the social engineer uses computer applications to trick users into carrying out a specific action. On the other hand, human based tactics are performed by attackers who understand flaws in human psychology. Businesses should be conscious of both categories of social engineering tactics because each approach could lead to a compromised network. The following are various types of social engineering attacks but attackers are not limited to only these methods:

- **Baiting:** A hacker preloads malware onto external storage devices (i.e. CDs or USBs) and strategically leaves them in public areas of the targeted business. Unsuspecting employees then pick up these CDs or USBs labeled company info and plugs it into their computers.
- **Phishing:** Social engineers send fraudulent emails that may look legitimate to recipients. The email may request an action such as disclosing sensitive information or clicking a malicious link.
- **Pretexting:** The malicious actors use masquerading and dishonesty to retrieve valuable information about the person or company. The attacker calls an employee and request him or her to validate their username and password for security purposes.
- **Quid pro quo:** The social engineer preforms a good deed for the victim in hopes of gaining their gratitude. The victim is then more likely to return the favor with a favor.
- **Tailgating:** The malicious actor waits near an entrance until authorized personnel enters and follows the employee into the controlled area.
- **Dumpster Diving:** Attackers rummage through a company's dumpster or trash cans with hopes of finding useful information about the company, its employees and the network.

III. RISE IN CYBERCRIME

Cybersecurity incidents are not only increasing in number, they are also becoming progressively destructive and target a broadening array of information and attack vectors (Beard, Mickelberg, Stapf, & Ulsch, 2015). Similar to business networks that are investing in technologies, sharing intelligence and training their employees so are cybercriminals. Malicious actors are persistently improving their tactics, techniques and procedures (TTPs) to become more effective at what they do. These threat actors have recognized how lucrative the cybercrime market is and are allocating resources to add more sophistication to their strategy. Social engineering enhances attack vectors by offering a polymorphic disguise that is detrimental to information security. Attackers incorporate social engineering techniques to execute initial reconnaissance, penetration, gaining a foothold, appropriating privileges and internal reconnaissance (Kostadinov, 2013). This allow perpetrators to exploit more weaknesses and sustain a longer presence on a compromised network. Both of which have contributed to a spike in success rates and increase in cybercrime. Below are some statistics presented in the 2015 ISACA and RSA Conference Survey that identifies the types of threat actors and successful attacks reported in 2014.

Threat Actors of 2014 (636 Respondents)

- 45.6% Cybercriminals
- 40.72% Non-malicious insiders
- 40.09% Hackers
- 28.62% Malicious insiders
- 19.81% Hacktivists
- 17.45% Nation State

Successful Attack Types of 2014 (704 Respondents)

- 68.32% Phishing
- 66.48% Malware
- 50.14% Hacking attempts
- 46.45% Social engineering
- 43.89% Loss of mobile devices
- 25.28% Insider theft
- 21.88% SQL injections
- 11.08% Man-in-the-Middle attacks
- 7.53% Watering hole

IV. PREVENTING SOCIAL ENGINEERING

It is evident that regardless of how technologically secure a network seems the human element will always be a vulnerability. The success rate and number of cybercrimes are steadily on the rise due to the level of anonymity social engineering offers malicious actors. Businesses have to remain cognitive of the various threat actors and their plethora of attacks so they are able to respond accordingly. There are technical and non-technical safeguards that can be implemented to lower the risk associated with social engineering to a tolerable level. Companies are adding multiple layers to their security schemes so that if the mechanism in the outer layer fails, a mechanism in at least one inner layer can help prevent a threat from turning into a disaster (Risk Mitigation). This concept is known as Multi-Layer Defense or Defense in Depth. A good Defense in Depth structure includes a mixture of the following precautionary measures:

- **Security Policy:** A well written policy should include technical and nontechnical approaches that are downward driven by executive management. Every organization should integrate security into their operational objectives.

- **Education and Training:** Employees ought to be required to attend initial training during orientation and recurring refresher trainings. This builds awareness by exposing users to commonly employed tactics and behaviors targeted by a social engineer.
- **Network Guidance:** The organization have to safeguard the network by whitelisting authorized websites, using Network address translation (NAT), and disabling unused applications and ports. Network users have to maintain complex passwords that are changed every 60 days.
- **Audits and Compliance:** Organizations have to actively verify that their security policy is being adhered to. Some detective controls include reviewing network logs, re-validating employees' permissions, and checking desktop configurations at least bi-monthly.
- **Technical Procedures:** The network should have multiple layers of defense to protect data and core infrastructure. Software like Intrusion Prevention Systems (IPS), Intrusion Detection Systems (IDS) and firewalls should be installed on every device. Demilitarized Zones (DMZ), web filters and Virtual Private Network (VPN) should be installed on all external facing services.
- **Physical Guidance:** There are a range of options that can be implemented to protect physical assets. Using a combination of security guards, mantraps and security cameras to deter intruders from entering the premises is beneficial. In places where physical hardware is located businesses should employ multifactor authentication, biometrics or access control list before access is granted.

V. CONCLUSION

In summary, social engineering is not something that is new but is a skill of deception that has been used for years. The world continues to grow technologically dependent and malicious actors are anxious to exploit this dependency in order to gain the monetary profit or recognition they desire. The expansion of smartphones and social media has provided cybercriminals with new avenues of attack which they have taken full advantage of. Cyberattacks have become so prevalent because social engineering is hard to detect and can be added to various attack vectors. Both sides are investing lots of time, money and other resources in effort to defeat one another in a Digital War where the environment is ever changing. Unfortunately, social engineering has reemerged and has proven to be just as effective in the 21st Century as it was in the past.

REFERENCES

Beard, C., Mickelberg, K., Stapf, E., & Ulsch, D. (2015, July). US cybersecurity: Progress stalled. *PWC*, 3. Retrieved from https://www.pwc.com/cybersecurity

Course Material: Risk Mitigation: Defense in Depth. (n.d.). University of Maryland University College. Retrieved from https://learn.umuc.edu/d2l/le/content/133521/viewContent/4176011/View

Information Systems Audit and Control Association & Rivest Shamir Adleman. (2015). State of cybersecurity: Implications for 2015. *Cybersecurity Nexus*. Retrieved from https://www.isaca.org/cyber/Documents/State-of-Cybersecurity

Kostadinov, D. (2013, March 22). The cyber exploitation life cycle. *InfoSec Institute*. Retrieved from http://www.resources.infosecinstitute.com

Peters, S. (2015, March 17). The 7 best social engineering attacks ever. *Information Week*, 1. http://www.darkreading.com

Rouse, M. (2014, November). Social engineering definition. *TechTarget*. Retrieved from http://searchsecurity.techtarget.com

Thapar, A. (n.d.). Social Engineering - An attack vector most intricate to tackle. *CISSP*. Retrieved from http://www.infosecwriters.com

Compilation of References

Ellis. (n.d.). Ethical Hacking. In *Computer and Information Security Handbook* (pp. 475-481). doi:10.1016/B978-0-12-803843-7.00030-2

Mitnick, K. D., & Simon, W. L. (2011). *Ghost in the wires: My adventures as the world's most wanted hacker*. Back Bay Books.

Hero, C. (n.d.). *Man in the Middle Attack*. Retrieved from: https://www.coursehero.com/file/ p3u2v5p/Man-in-the-middle-MitM-attack-A-MitM-attack-occurs-when-a-hacker-inserts-itself/

Pagliery, J. (2014, May 28). *Half of American adults hacked this year*. Retrieved from https:// money.cnn.com/2014/05/28/technology/security/hack-data-breach/

Ponemon Institute. (2015, May). *2015 Cost of data breach study: United States*. Retrieved from IBM website: http://public.dhe.ibm.com/common/ssi/ecm/se/en/sew03055usen/SEW03055USEN.PDF

Simon, G. K. (2010). *In sheep's clothing: Understanding and dealing with manipulative people* (2nd ed.). Parkurst Brothers.

Statista. (2015, August). *Number of compromised data records in selected data breaches as of August 2015*. Retrieved from https://www.statista.com/statistics/290525/cyber-crime-biggest-online-data-breaches-worldwide/

Yang, J. L., & Jayakumar, A. (2014, January 10). *Target says up to 70 million more customers were hit by December data breach*. Retrieved from https://www.washingtonpost.com/business/ economy/target-says-70-million-customers-were-hit-by-dec-data-breach-more-than-first-reported/2014/01/10/0ada1026-79fe-11e3-8963-b4b654bcc9b2_story.html

Braiker, H. B. (2004). *Who's pulling your strings?: How to break the cycle of manipulation and regain control of your life*. McGraw-Hill.

Merriam-Webster. (n.d.). Security. *Merriam-webster online*. Accessed 18 October 2018 from www.m-w.com/dictionary/security

Standard Occupational Classification System. (2020, April 17). Retrieved July 21, 2020, from https://www.bls.gov/soc/2018/major_groups.htm#15-0000

Compilation of References

Curry, S. J. J. (2013). Instant-messaging security. In J. Vacca (Ed.), *Computer and information security handbook* (2nd ed., p. 727). Morgan Kaufmann. doi:10.1016/B978-0-12-803843-7.00051-X

Notes, M. C. (2015). *Information Security – Evolution.* Retrieved from: https://thisismyclassnotes. blogspot.com/2015/06/information-security-evolution.html

Enterprise Risk Management. (2009, November). *Social engineering: People hacking.* Retrieved from https://www.emrisk.com/sites/default/files/newsletters/ERMNewsletter_november_2009.pdf

National Security Telecommunications and Information Systems Security. (1994). *National Training Standard for Information Systems Security (Infosec) Professionals.* Author.

Felson, M., & Clarke, R. V. (1998). *Opportunity makes the thief: Practical theory for crime prevention* (Police Research Series Paper 98). Retrieved from https://webarchive.nationalarchives. gov.uk/20110218135832/rds.homeoffice.gov.uk/rds/prgpdfs/fprs98.pdf

Javat Point. (n.d.a). *Cyber Security Introduction.* Retrieved from: https://www.javatpoint. com/cyber-security-introduction#:~:text="Cybersecurity%20is%20 primarily%20about%20 people,including%20computer%20network%20operations%2C%20information

Granger, S. (2010, November 3). *Social engineering fundamentals, part 1: Hacker tactics.* Retrieved from https://www.symantec.com/connect/articles/social-engineering-fundamentals-part-i-hacker-tactics

Javat Point. (n.d.b). *Cyber Security Principles.* Retrieved from: https://www.javatpoint.com/cyber-security-principles

CIO Wiki. (n.d.). *Disaster Recovery Plan (DRP).* Retrieved from: https://cio-wiki.org/wiki/Disaster_Recovery_Plan_(DRP)

Grover, R., Hosenball, M., & Finkle, J. (2014, December 3). *Sony Pictures struggles to recover eight days after cyber attack.* Retrieved from https://www.reuters.com/article/2014/12/03/us-sony-cybersecurity-investigation-idUSKCN0JG27B20141203

Kumar, A. (2019). *Cyber Security.* Retrieved from: https://www.linkedin.com/pulse"/cyber-security-amar-kumar/

Internet Live Stats. (2014, July 1). *Internet users in the world.* Retrieved from https://www. internetlivestats.com/internet-users/

Smurf, R. (2015). *The 5 Phases of a Phishing Attack.* Retrieved from: https://www.cybrary.it/blog/0p3n/anatomy-of-the-hack/

Gur, Bahtiyar, & Algoz. (2015). Security analysis of computer networks. In *Modeling Simulation of Computer Networks and Systems.* Elsevier.

Kim, P. (2014). *The hacker playbook: Practical guide to penetration testing.* Secure Planet.

A. B. (1994). Image compression using the discrete cosine transform. *The Mathematica Journal, 4*(1), 81–88.

Abdelwahab, A. A., & Hassaan, L. A. (2008). A discrete wavelet transform based technique for image data hiding. *2008 National Radio Science Conference, 1*(1), 1-9. 10.1109/NRSC.2008.4542319

Acquisdata Industry Profile. (2020b). *Cybersecurity Industry*. Acquisdata Global Industry SnapShot Cybersecurity Industry.

Acquisdata Industry Profile: Artificial Intelligence Software Industry. (2020a). Acquisdata Global Industry SnapShot. *Artificial Intelligence Software Industry, 295*, 1–48.

Alex, M. E., & Kishore, R. (2017). Forensics framework for cloud computing. *Computers & Electrical Engineering, 60*, 193–205. https://doig.org/10.1016/j.compeleceng.2017.02.006

Allen, M. (2006). *Social engineering. A means to violate a computer system*. Academic Press.

Al-Muhtadi, J., Shahzad, B., Saleem, K., Jameel, W., & Orgun, M. A. (2019). Cybersecurity and privacy issues for socially integrated mobile healthcare applications operating in a multi-cloud environment. *Health Informatics Journal, 25*(2), 315–329. doi:10.1177/1460458217706184 PMID:28480788

Anderson, K. E. (2020). Getting acquainted with social networks and apps: It is time to talk about TikTok. *Library Hi Tech News, 37*(4), 7–12. doi:10.1108/LHTN-01-2020-0001

Andress, J. (2011). *The Basics of Information Security*. Elsevier.

Anonymous. (2013). *FBI: Cyber-attacks surpassing terrorism as major domestic threat*. Retrieved from https://www.rt.com/usa/fbi-cyber-attack-threat-739/

Arce, D. G. (2020). Cybersecurity and platform competition in the cloud. *Computers & Security, 93*, 101774. Advance online publication. doi:10.1016/j.cose.2020.101774

Artificial Intelligence Software. Market Report. (2019). In *Artificial Intelligence Software*. Acquisdata, Inc. https://bi-gale-com.ezproxy.umgc.edu/global/article/GALE%7CA601435798?u=umd_umuc&sid=ebsco

Assignment help - high QUALITY Assignment help in Australia. (2019). Retrieved March 27, 2021, from https://assignmenthelp4me.com/

Australia, D. D. L. S. (2019). *Meeting Australia's cyber security challenge*. DDLS Australia. Retrieved July 28, 2020, from https://www.ddls.com.au/wp-content/uploads/2019/08/DDLS-ebook-August-2019-Final.pdf

Badescu, I., & Dumitrescu, C. (2014). Steganography in image using discrete wavelet transformation. *Advances in Mathematical Models and Production Systems in Engineering, 1*(313), 69–72.

Baldwin, J., Alhawi, O. M., Shaughnessy, S., Akinbi, A., & Dehghantanha, A. (2018). Emerging from the cloud: A bibliometric analysis of cloud forensics studies. *Advances in Information Security Cyber Threat Intelligence, 70*, 311–331. https://doig.org/10.1007/978-3-319-73951-9_16

Compilation of References

Beard, C., Mickelberg, K., Stapf, E., & Ulsch, D. (2015, July). US cybersecurity: Progress stalled. *PWC*, 3. Retrieved from https://www.pwc.com/cybersecurity

Bisson, D. (2015, Mar 23). 5 Social Engineering Attacks to Watch Out For. *The State of Security*. Retrieved from https://www.tripwire.com/state-of-security/security-awareness/5-social-engineering-attacks-to-watch-out-for/

Bowen, B. M., Devarajan, R., & Stolfo, S. (2011). Measuring the Human Factor of Cyber Security. *Columbia University*. Retrieved from http://www.cs.columbia.edu/~bmbowen/papers/metrics_hst.pdf

Braiker, H. B. (2004). *Who's pulling your strings? How to break the cycle of manipulation and regain control of your life*. McGraw-Hill.

Bucerzan, D., Rațiu, C., & Manolescu, M. (2013). SmartSteg: A new android based steganography application. *International Journal of Computers, Communications & Control, 8*(5), 681. doi:10.15837/ijccc.2013.5.642

Bunker, G. (2020). Tik-Tok Danger. *Network Security, 2020*(1), 3–3. doi:10.1016/S1353-4858(20)30004-0

Certified ethical hacker: InfoSec cyber Security Certification: EC-Council. (2016). Retrieved March 27, 2021, from https://www.eccouncil.org/

Chen, S., Zhao, S., Han, B., & Wang, X. (2019). 2019 wireless days (wd). In Investigating and revealing privacy leaks in mobile application traffic (pp. 1–4). IEEE. doi:10.1109/WD.2019.8734246

Chen, P.Y. & JuLin, H. (2006). A DWT based approach for image steganography. *International Journal of Applied Science and Engineering., 1*(1), 275–290.

Chitery. A., Singh, D., Bag, M., & Singh, V. (2012). A Comprehensive Study of Social Engineering Based Attacks in India to Develop a Conceptual Model. *International Journal of Information & Network Security, 1*(2), 45-53.

Choo, K.-K. R., Bishop, M., Glisson, W., & Nance, K. (2018). Internet- and cloud-of-things cybersecurity research challenges and advances. *Computers & Security, 74*, 275–276. doi:10.1016/j.cose.2018.02.008

Cisco Press. (2013). Retrieved March 27, 2021, from https://www.ciscopress.com/articles/article.asp?p=1998559

Cloud Security Alliance. (2017). *Cloud Security Alliance's Security Guidance for Critical Areas of Focus in Cloud Computing*. https://cloudsecurityalliance.org/artifacts/security-guidance-v4/

Cobb, M. J. (2018). Plugging the skills gap: The vital role that women should play in cyber security. *Computer Fraud & Security, 2018*(1), 5–8. https://doig.org/10.1016/s1361-3723(18)30004-6

CompTIA. (2020). *What Is SaaS*. https://www.comptia.org/content/articles/what-is-saas

Costa, D. G., & Guedes, L. A. (2012). A discrete wavelet transform (dwt)-based energy-efficient selective retransmission mechanism for wireless image sensor networks. *Journal of Sensor and Actuator Networks, 1*(3), 3–35. doi:10.3390/jsan1010003

Course Material: Risk Mitigation: Defense in Depth. (n.d.). University of Maryland University College. Retrieved from https://learn.umuc.edu/d2l/le/content/133521/viewContent/4176011/View

Course Overview. (2020). *Johnstone High School – Computing and Junior Education.* Retrieved March 27, 2021, from http://cybersecurity.jhigh.co.uk/index.html

Currie, D. (2003). *Shedding some light on Voice Authentication.* SANS Institute. Retrieved from: https://www.sans.org/reading-room/whitepapers/authentication/shedding-light-voice-authentication-847

Diana, A. (2015, May 19). *Social Engineering Targets Weakest Security Link: Employees.* Retrieved from http://www.enterprisetech.com/2015/05/19/social-engineering-targets-weakest-security-link-employees/

Dong, J. Q., Wu, W., & Zhang, Y. (2018). The faster the better? Innovation speed and user interest in open source software. *Information & Management.* https://doi-org.ezproxy.umgc.edu/10.1016/j.im.2018.11.002

Doshi, R., Jain, P., & Lalit Gupta, L. (2012). Steganography and its applications in security. *International Journal of Modern Engineering Research, 2*(6), 4635.

Dykstra, J., & Sherman, A. T. (2013). Design and implementation of FROST: Digital forensic tools for the OpenStack cloud computing platform. *Digital Investigation, 10*(Supplement), S87–S95. https://doi.org/10.1016/j.diin.2013.06.010

Engebretson, P. (2011). *The Basics of Hacking and Penetration Testing.* Elsevier.

Enisa. (2016). *Vulnerabilities and Exploits.* Retrieved March 24, 2021 https://www.enisa.europa.eu/topics/csirts-in-europe/glossary/vulnerabilities-and-exploits

Ethical hacking and countermeasures. (2017). Cengage Learning.

Faheem, K., & Rafique, K. (2015). Securing 4g/5g wireless networks. *Computer Fraud & Security, 2015*(5), 8–12. doi:10.1016/S1361-3723(15)30036-1

Fraud risk and cybercrime on the rise. (2014). *Money Marketing,* 29.

Gartner Inc. (2021). *Fueling the future of business.* Retrieved March 27, 2021, from https://www.gartner.com/en

Compilation of References

Gartner. (2019, November 13). *Gartner Forecasts Worldwide Public Cloud Revenue to Grow 17% in 2020* [Press release]. https://www.gartner.com/en/newsroom/press-releases/2019-11-13-gartner-forecasts-worldwide-public-cloud-revenue-to-grow-17-percent-in-2020#:~:text=Software%20 as%20a%20service%20(SaaS,software%20(see%20Table%201).&text=IaaS%20is%20 forecast%20to%20grow,rate%20across%20all%20market%20segments.

Gautam, B. (2010). *Image compression using discrete cosine transform & discrete wavelet transform.* Bachelor of Technology Degree in Computer Science and Engineering at the National Institute of Technology, Rourkela (Deemed University). http://ethesis.nitrkl.ac.in/1731/1/project.pdf

Goodchild, J. (2012, December 20). *Social engineering: the basics.* Retrieved November 2, 2015, from https://www.csoonline.com/article/2124681/security-awareness/social-engineering-the-basics.html

Griffin, T. (2020, May 21). *Cybersecurity trends in 2020 & the threats facing the industry.* Retrieved July 21, 2020, from https://blog.eccouncil.org/cybersecurity-trends-in-2020-the-threats-facing-the-industry/

Grimes, R. (2019, February 27). *What is ethical hacking? How to get paid to break into computers.* Retrieved March 27, 2021, from https://www.csoonline.com/article/3238128/what-is-ethical-hacking-and-how-to-become-an-ethical-hacker.html

Grimes, R. A. (2015). 5 Reasons Internet Crime is Worse Than Ever. *Info World.* Retrieved From https://www.infoworld.com/article/2608631/security/5-reasons-internet-crime-is-worse-than-ever.html?page=2

Gupta, R., Tanwar, S., Tyagi, S., & Kumar, N. (2019). Tactile internet and its applications in 5g era: A comprehensive review. *International Journal of Communication Systems, 32*(14), e3981. Advance online publication. doi:10.1002/dac.3981

Hassan. (2012). Cybercrime in Nigeria: Causes, Effects and the Way Out. *ARPN Journal of Science and Technology, 2*(7). Retrieved from: http://www.ejournalofscience.org/archive/vol2no7/vol2no7_11.pdf

Heary, J. (n.d.). *Top 5 social engineering exploit techniques.* Retrieved November 2, 2015, from https://www.pcworld.com/article/182180

Heimdal Security - Proactive Cyber Security Software. (n.d.). Retrieved March 28, 2021, from https://heimdalsecurity.com/en/

Hemalatha, S. (2013). A Secure Color Image Steganography in Transform Domain. *International Journal on Cryptography and Information Security, 3*(1), 17–24. doi:10.5121/ijcis.2013.3103

Herman, M., Iorga, M., Landreville, N., Lee, R., Mishra, A., Sardinas, R., & Wang, Y. (2020, August). *NISTIR 8006: NIST Cloud Computing Forensic Science Challenges.* Retrieved September 6, 2020, from doi:10.6028/NIST.IR.8006

Hewes, J. A. (2016). Threat and Challenges of Cyber-Crime and the Response. *SAM Advanced Management Journal, 81*(2), 4-10.

HITRUST Alliance. (2020, August). *Introduction to the HITRUST CSF*. https://hitrustalliance. net/content/uploads/CSFv9.4_Introduction.pdf

Hong, J. B., Nhlabatsi, A., Kim, D. S., Hussein, A., Fetais, N., & Khan, K. M. (2019). Systematic identification of threats in the cloud: A survey. *Computer Networks*, *150*, 46–69. doi:10.1016/j. comnet.2018.12.009

Hoovers. (2020a). Industry Custom Report: IT Services in the United States. *Hoovers Research Database*. https://app-avention-com.ezproxy.umgc.edu/API/Report/ApplinkPDF/API/Custom/ GetIndustryReport.aspx?Report=MARKETRESEARCH&Type=GetReport&FileFormat=PD F&ReportID=60432&FileName=0072-2313-2019.pdf&VendorName=Datamonitor

Hoovers. (2020b). Industry Custom Report: Software in the United States. *Hoovers Research Database*. https://app-avention-com.ezproxy.umgc.edu/API/Report/ApplinkPDF/API/Custom/ GetIndustryReport.aspx?Report=MARKETRESEARCH&Type=GetReport&FileFormat=PD F&ReportID=60316&FileName=0072-0381-2019.pdf&VendorName=Datamonitor

Huang, M.-H., Rust, R., & Maksimovic, V. (2019). The Feeling Economy: Managing in the Next Generation of Artificial Intelligence (AI). *California Management Review*, *61*(4), 43–65. doi:10.1177/0008125619863436

Hussain, M. (2013). A survey of image steganography techniques. *International Journal of Advanced Science and Technology, 54*, 116-117.

Imprivata. (2016, February 23). *Imprivata expands authentication platform to protect medical devices and remote access to patient information from hacking* [Press release]. Retrieved September 7, 2020, from https://www.imprivata.com/company/press/imprivata-expands-authentication- platform-protect-medical-devices-and-remote-access

Incidents of Ransomware on the rise. (2016, July 14). Retrieved from https://www.fbi.gov/news/ stories/2016/april/incidents-of-ransomware-on-the-rise/incidents-ofransomware-on-the-rise

Information Systems Audit and Control Association & Rivest Shamir Adleman. (2015). State of cybersecurity: Implications for 2015. *Cybersecurity Nexus*. Retrieved from https://www.isaca. org/cyber/Documents/State-of-Cybersecurity

Iozzio, C. (2008, September 26). *The 10 most mysterious cyber crimes*. Retrieved November 2, 2015, from http://www.pcmag.com/article2/0,2817,2331225,00.asp

Jaret, P. (2018, November 12). *Exposing vulnerabilities: How hackers could target your medical devices*. Retrieved July 28, 2020, from https://www.aamc.org/news-insights/exposing- vulnerabilities-how-hackers-could-target-your-medical-devices

Jones, M. (2020). Stress testing the skills gap. *Computer Fraud & Security*, *2020*(5), 9–11. https:// doig.org/10.1016/s1361-3723(20)30051-8

Kociołek, M., Materka, A., Strzelecki, M., & Szczypiński, P. (2001). Discrete wavelet transform – derived features for digital image texture analysis. *International Conference on Signals and Electronic Systems*, 2.

Koochaksaraei, R., Aghazarian, V., Haroonabadi, A. &Hedayati, A. (2012). A novel data hiding method by using chaotic map and histogram. *International Journal of Innovation, Management and Technology, 3*(5), 642.

Kostadinov, D. (2013, March 22). The cyber exploitation life cycle. *InfoSec Institute*. Retrieved from http://www.resources.infosecinstitute.com

Kumar, V., & Kumar, D. (2010). Performance evaluation of DWT based image steganography. *2010 IEEE 2nd International Advance Computing Conference (IACC), 1*(1), 223-228. 10.1109/IADCC.2010.5423005

Kumar, A., & Pooja, K. (2010). Steganography- a data hiding technique. *International Journal of Computer Applications, 9*(7), 1–2.

Kumarpanjabi, P., & Singh, P. (2013). *An* enhanced data hiding approach using pixel mapping method with optimal substitution approach. *International Journal of Computer Applications, 74*(10), PP. 38.

Kumar, S. (2014). *Image steganography using improved LSB and EXOR encryption algorithm.* dspace.thapar.edu

Li, S., Pilcher, C., & Gepford, J. (2018). Cybersecurity war: A new front—Hospitals need to be proactive to prevent hacks of connected medical devices. *Trustee, 71*(6), 16.

Luo, X., Brody, R., Seazzu, A., & Burd, S. (2011). Social Engineering: The Neglected Human Factor for Information Security Management. *Information Resources Management Journal, 24*(3), 1–8.

Maharjan, S. K., & Qiaolun, G. (2014). Information hiding using image decomposing. *International Journal of Scientific Research, 3*(3), 73–76.

Mandal, J. (2012). Colour image steganography based on pixel value differencing in spatial domain. *International Journal of Information Sciences and Techniques, 2*(4), 84.

Mann, P. S., & Sharma, M. (2012). Social Engineering: A Partial Technical Attack. *IJCSI International Journal of Computer Science Issues, 9*(2), 557-559. Retrieved from http://citeseerx.ist.psu.edu/viewdoc/download?doi=10.1.1.401.7920&rep=rep1&type=pdf

Matthews, K. (2020, January 2). *3 healthcare cybersecurity trends to watch in 2020.* Retrieved July 21, 2020, from https://hitconsultant.net/2020/01/02/3-healthcare-cybersecurity- trends-to-watch-in-2020/#.XxeK1J5KhPY

Maze ransomware Attacks Us It Firm. (2020). Retrieved March 28, 2021, from https://www.trendmicro.com/vinfo/us/security/news/cybercrime-and-digital-threats/maze-ransomware-attacks-us-it-firm

McAfee. (2014). *Net Losses: Estimating the Global Cost of Cybercrime Economic impact of cybercrime II.* Center for Strategic and International Studies.

McGee, M., & Ross, R. (2017, January 10). *A new in-depth analysis of Anthem breach.* Retrieved September 7, 2020, from https://www.bankinfosecurity.com/new-in-depth-analysis-anthem-breach-a-9627

Mercer, E. (n.d.). *Causes of cyber crime.* Retrieved November 2, 2015, from http://science.opposingviews.com/causes-cyber-crime-1846.html

Mickelberg, K., Pollard, N., & Schive, L. (2014). *US cybercrime: rising risks, reduce readiness.* Retrieved November 2, 2015, from https://www.pwc.com/us/en/increasing-it-effectiveness/publications/assets/2014-us-state-of-cybercrime.pdf

Micro, T. (2012). *Spear-Phishing Email: Most Favored APT Attack Bait.* Trend Micro. http://www. trendmicro.com.au/cloud-content/us/pdfs/security-intelligence/whitepapers/wp-spear-phishing-email-most-favored-apt-attackbait.pdf

Mishra, M., & Adhikary, M. C. (2014). Detection of clones in digital images. *International Journal of Computer Science and Business Informatics, 9*(1), 91–101.

Mistry, I., Tanwar, S., Tyagi, S., & Kumar, N. (2020). Blockchain for 5g-enabled iot for industrial automation: A systematic review, solutions, and challenges. *Mechanical Systems and Signal Processing, 135*, 106382. Advance online publication. doi:10.1016/j.ymssp.2019.106382

Mitras, B. A., & Aboo, A. (2013). Proposed steganography approach using DNA properties. *International Journal of Information Technology and Business Management, 14*(1), 79.

Mohr, T. (2018, March 2). *Why women don't apply for jobs unless they're 100% qualified.* Retrieved September 17, 2020, from https://hbr.org/2014/08/why-women-dont-apply-for-jobs-unless-theyre-100-qualified

Mousa, H., Moustafa, K., Abdel-Wahed, W., & Hadhoud, M. (2011). Data hiding based on contrast mapping using DNA medium. *The International Arab Journal of Information Technology, 8*(2), 148.

Mstafa, R., & Bac, C. (2013). Information hiding in images using steganography techniques. *ASEE Northeast Section Conference Norwich University, 1*(1), 1–8.

NAICS Code 541513: Computer facilities management services. (n.d.). Retrieved July 21, 2020, from https://www.naics.com/naics-code-description/?code=541513

Nakashima, E., & Peterson, A. (2014, June 9). Report: Cybercrime and espionage costs $445 billion annually. *The Washington Post.* Retrieved from https://www.washingtonpost.com/world/national-security/report-cybercrime-and-espionage-costs-445-billion-annually/2014/06/08/8995291c-ecce-11e3-9f5c-9075d5508f0a_story.html

Narasimmalou, T., & Joseph, A. R. (2012). Discrete Wavelet Transform Based Steganography for Transmitting Images. *IEEE-International Conference on Advances In Engineering, Science And Management*, 370-375.

Nasereddin, H. O. (2011). Digital watermarking a technology overview. *IJRRAS, 6*(1), 89–91.

Nelson, J., Lin, X., Chen, C., Iglesias, J., & Li, J. J. (2016). Social Engineering for Security Attacks. *ACM International Conference Proceeding Series, 1*. doi:10.1145/2955129.2955158

Netwrix. (2021). *Powerful data security made easy*. Retrieved March 27, 2021, from https://www.netwrix.com/

Norton. (n.d.). *The Definition of cybercrime*. Retrieved November 2, 2015, from https://us.norton.com/cybercrime-definition/promo

Pagliery, J. (2014). *Bitcoin: And the Future of Money*. Academic Press.

Pagliery, J. (2014, May 28). *Half of American adults hacked this year*. Retrieved from https://money.cnn.com/2014/05/28/technology/security/hack-data-breach/

Parul, M., & Rohil, H. (2014). Optimized Image Steganography using Discrete Wavelet Transform (DWT). *International Journal of Recent Development in Engineering and Technology, 2*(2), 75–81.

Peters, S. (2015 March 17) Information Week, *The Seven Best Social Engineering Attacks Ever*. https://www.darkreading.com/the-7-best-social-engineering-attacks-ever/d/d-id/1319411

Peters, S. (2015, March 17). The 7 best social engineering attacks ever. *Information Week*, 1. http://www.darkreading.com

Pew Research Center. (2020). *Cyber Attacks Likely to Increase*. Retrieved from: https://www.pewinternet.org/2014/10/29/cyber-attacks-likely-to-increase/

Ponemon Institute. (2015, May). *2015 Cost of data breach study: United States*. Retrieved from IBM website: http://public.dhe.ibm.com/common/ssi/ecm/se/en/sew03055usen/SEW03055USEN.PDF

Provos, N., & Honeyman, P. (2003). Hide and seek: An introduction to steganography. *IEEE Secur. Privacy Mag., 1*(3), 32–44. doi:10.1109/MSECP.2003.1203220

Ragan, S. (2013). Social Engineering: Study finds Americans willingly open malicious emails. *CSO*. Retrieved from https://www.csoonline.com/article/2133877/social-engineering/social-engineering--study-finds-americans-willingly-open-malicious-emails.html

Rao, S. K., & Prasad, R. (2018). Impact of 5g technologies on industry 4.0. *Wireless Personal Communications: An International Journal, 100*(1), 145–159. doi:10.100711277-018-5615-7

Reasons for the rise in cyber crime in Nigeria. (n.d.). Retrieved November 2, 2015, from https://martinslibrary.blogspot.com/2013/08/reasons-for-rise-in-cyber-crime-in.html

Richardson, R., & North, M. (2017). Ransomware: Evolution, Mitigation and Prevention. *International Management Review, 13*(1), 10–21.

Rouse, M. (2014, November). Social engineering definition. *TechTarget*. Retrieved from http://searchsecurity.techtarget.com

Rouse, M. (2015). *Social engineering*. Retrieved from https://searchsecurity.techtarget.com/definition/social-engineerring

Savage, K., Coogan, P., & Lau, H. (2015). *The Evolution of Ransomware*. Academic Press.

Schiff, J. L. (2013 June 19). *15 Ways to Protect Your Ecommerce Site From Hacking and Fraud.* http://www.cio.com/article/2384809/e-commerce/15-ways-to-protect-your-ecommerce-site-from-hacking-and-fraud.html

Seigfried-Spellar, K. C., Rogers, M. K., & Crimmins, D. M. (2017). Development of a professional code of ethics in digital forensics. In *Proceedings of the Conference on Digital Forensics, Security & Law* (pp. 135–144). Academic Press.

Sheth, R. K., & Tank, R. M. (2015). Image steganography techniques. *International Journal of Computational Engineering Science, 1*(1), 10–11.

Shobana, M., & Manikandan, R. (2013). Efficient method for hiding data by pixel intensity. *International Journal of Engineering and Technology, 5*(1), 75.

Shuang, Z., Xiapu, L., Xiaobo, M., Bo, B., Yankang, Z., Wei, Z., ... Xinliang, Q. (2018). (2018). Exploiting proximity-based mobile apps for large-scale location privacy probing. *Security and Communication Networks, 2018*, 1–22. Advance online publication. doi:10.1155/2018/3182402

Smith, S. W. (1999). The discrete Fourier transform. *The Scientist and Engineer's Guide to Digital Signal Processing*, 145. https://www.dspguide.com/ch8.htm

Sravanthi, G.S., Devi, B.S., Riyazoddin, S.M., & Reddy, M. J. (2012). A spatial domain image steganography technique based on plane bit substitution method. *Global Journal of Computer Science and Technology Graphics & Vision, 12*, 2-3.

Srinivasa Raghavan, R., Jayasimha, K. R., & Rajendra, V. N. (2020). Impact of software as a service (SaaS) on software acquisition process. *Journal of Business & Industrial Marketing, 35*(4), 757–770. https://doi-org.ezproxy.umgc.edu/10.1108/JBIM-12-2018-0382

State of Ransomware 2016: Understanding the Depth of the Ransomware Problem in the United States. (2016). Osterman Research, Inc.

Statista. (2015, August). *Number of compromised data records in selected data breaches as of August 2015*. Retrieved from https://www.statista.com/statistics/290525/cyber-crime-biggest-online-data-breachesworldwide/

Statista. (2015, August). *Number of compromised data records in selected data breaches as of August 2015*. Retrieved from https://www.statista.com/statistics/290525/cyber-crime-biggest-online-data-breaches-worldwide/

Strohm, C. (2014). Cyber Theft, Already a 445 Billion Business, to Grow Bigger. *Insurance Journal.* Retrieved https://www.insurancejournal.com/news/national/2014/06/09/331333.htm

Sumathi, C.P., Santanam, T. & Umamaheswari, G. (2014). A study of various steganographic techniques used for information hiding. *International Journal of Computer Science & Engineering Survey, 4*(6), 10-11. 4. doi:10.5121/ijcses.2013.4602

Compilation of References

Surge in Cyberattacks Leaves Economic Impact on U.S. State and Local Governments By CISOMAG. (2020). https://cisomag.eccouncil.org/magazine/

Swinhoe, D. (2020, April 17). *The 15 biggest data breaches of the 21st century.* CSO Online. https://www.csoonline.com/article/2130877/the-biggest-data-breaches-of-the-21st-century.html

Synopsis: Open Source Security and Risk Analysis. (2018). *Network Security, 3*(6). https://doi-org.ezproxy.umgc.edu/10.1016/S1353-4858(18)30051-5

Synopsys. (2020). Synopsys 2020 Open Source Security and Risk Analysis Report. *Synopsys.* https://www.synopsys.com/content/dam/synopsys/sig-assets/reports/2020-ossra-report.pdf

Sysel, P., & Rajmic, P. (2012). Goertzel algorithm generalized to non-integer multiples of fundamental frequency. *EURASIP Journal on Advances in Signal Processing, 2012*(1), 1.

Taylor, R. W., Fritsch, E. J., & Liederbach, J. (2015). *Digital Crime and Digital Terrorism* (3rd ed.). Pearson Education.

Thampi, S. M. (2004). Information hiding techniques: a tutorial review. ISTE-STTP on Network Security & Cryptography, LBSCE, 1-3.

Thapar, A. (n.d.). Social Engineering - An attack vector most intricate to tackle. *CISSP.* Retrieved from http://www.infosecwriters.com

The official social engineering portal - security through education. (2015). Retrieved November 2, 2015, from https://www.social-engineer.org/

Thompson, S. C. (2006). Helping the Hacker? Library Information, Security, and Social Engineering. *Information Technology and Libraries, 25*(4), 222–225. doi:10.6017/ital.v25i4.3355

Tiwari, A., Yadav, S. R., & Mittal, N.K. (2014). A review on different image steganography techniques. *International Journal of Engineering and Innovative Technology, 3*(7), 122.

Turban, E., Volonino, L., & Wood, G. (2020). *Information Technology For Management: Digital Strategies for Insight, Action, and Sustainable Performance* (10th ed.). John Wiley & Sons, Inc.

US cybercrime: Rising risks, reduced readiness. (2018). *US State of cybercrime Survey.* https://collabra.email/wp-content/uploads/2015/04/2014-us-state-of-cybercrime.pdf

Vacca, J. R. (2013). *Computer and Information Security* (2nd ed.). Kaufmann.

Vijay, M., & Vigneshkumar, V. (2013). Image steganography algorithm based on Huffman encoding and transform domain method. *2013 Fifth International Conference on Advanced Computing (ICoAC)*, 517. 10.1109/ICoAC.2013.6922005

Vulnerabilities, C. (2017). Article. *Credit Union Magazine, 83*(1), 15.

Webopedia. (2021). *What is Social Engineering?* Retrieved March 24, 2021 https://www.webopedia.com/definitions/social-engineering/

What Is Social Engineering: Attack Techniques & Prevention Methods: Imperva. (2019, December 29). Retrieved March 28, 2021, from https://www.imperva.com/learn/application-security/social-engineering-attack/

Youth Incorporated Magazine. (2020). *Ethical Hacking: A New Age IT Career For You*. Retrieved March 24, 2021 https://youthincmag.com/ethical-hacking-a-new-age-it-career-

Zetter, K. (2015, September 17). *Hacker lexicon: A guide to Ransomware, the scary hack that's on the rise*. Retrieved from Security: https://www.wired.com/2015/09/hacker-lexicon-guideransomware-scary-hack-thats-rise/Zetter

About the Contributors

Nabie Y. Conteh is a Computer Information Systems Professor at Southern University at New Orleans (SUNO). He holds a BS in information systems from the Institute for Information and Communication Technology, in the Netherlands; an MBA in information systems management from Ferris State University; and an MS and Ph.D. in information systems from the University of Maryland, Baltimore County. His areas of teaching and research interest include decision support systems, systems modeling and simulation; systems analysis and design; and knowledge management and organizational learning. Dr. Conteh possesses many technical skills and the ability to speak English, Dutch, Russian and German. Dr. Conteh has made presentations at national and international conferences and has been published in many refereed journals and proceedings. He has worked as Assistant Professor at Shenandoah University, as Associate Professor of Computer Information systems at West Liberty University, Ohio State University Eastern, as Adjunct Professor of Cyber Security at the Graduate School of the University of Maryland University College and Professor of Information Security and Global Information Technology at Florida Tech. During the tenure of his Ph.D. Program, he worked as Research Assistant at the University of Maryland Baltimore County. He did consulting for Datastream at College Park in Maryland, a company whose primary activity is data conversion. He had also worked for Getronics Transaction Services and EuroShell International, the ABN AMRO Bank at Amsterdam, in the Netherlands.

* * *

C. V. Anchugam has received her Ph.D in Network Security, P.G. and Research Department of Computer Science, at Government Arts College (Autonomous), Karur, Bharathidasan University, Tamilnadu, India. She has received her B.Sc (Computer Science) degree from Sri Saradha College of Arts and Science, Karur, Tamilnadu, India in 2002. She has received her M.C.A degree from M. Kumarasamy College of Engineering, Karur, Tamilnadu, India in 2005.She has published number of papers in esteemed national/international conferences and journals. Her interests are in Cryptography, Network security and Ad hoc networks.

Sahar Abd El Rahman has received her M.Sc. (2003) in an AI Technique Applied to Machine Aided Translation, and PhD (2008) in Reconstruction of High-Resolution Image from a Set of Low-Resolution Images, from the Faculty of Engineering- Shoubra, Benha University, Cairo, Egypt. She is currently Assistant Professor, College of Computer and Information System, Princess Nourah Bint Abdulrahman University (Saudia Arabia). Also, she is Assistant Professor from 2008 till now at Faculty of Engineering-Shoubra, Benha University, Cairo, Egypt. She has published many papers in national and international journals and conferences. Her research interests include Computer Vision, Image Processing, Signal Processing, Information Security, Human Computer Interaction, E-Health, Big Data and Cloud Computing.

Alusine Jalloh is a recent graduate from the University of Maryland, College Park with a degree in Family Science from the School of Public health, with a concentration in Family Therapy and Psychology. Alusine possesses a professional background in hospitality management, with a variety of experience managing front office departments in different brands, market areas, and demographics. He has translated his exceptional interpersonal skills and organizational skills gained from his professional experience into innovative ideas as a graduate student passionate about Cybersecurity. In the future, he hopes to utilize social engineering and penetration testing as a Cybersecurity consultant to work with companies closely in developing key strategies that bolsters their protection against vulnerabilities from external entities wishing to compromise & exploit valuable intellectual property along with the personal identifiable information of clients and their employees.

Alicia Leslie-Jones enlisted in the United States Navy in 2007 and served as a Signals Intelligence Analyst and Reporter until 2016. She received her BS in Information Technology from American Military University in 2019. She is currently a student at University of Maryland Global Campus pursuing a MS in Digital Forensics and Cyber Investigations and employed as a Senior Systems Administrator for ARMA-Global, A General Dynamics Information Technology Company.

Paul J. Schmick is a Speaker, Professor and Vice President of Security Technology for Alliance Security Services headquartered in New York. He joined Alliance in January 2016, and has 20 years of experience in the security and technology industries. Paul is a seasoned professional in the disciplines of security convergence and information technology, cybersecurity, physical security, risk-based security and security technologies. Previous to his appointment at Alliance, Paul served as the Director of Corporate Security Programs at FJC Security Services where he directed the company's corporate security programs, managed FJC's Office of Information Technology (OIT), and was the Managing Director of FJC Technology Solutions where he directed the organizations security technology and managed service division. Paul also served eight years with the U.S. Department of Homeland Security (DHS) - Transportation Security Administration (TSA), and was stationed at John F. Kennedy International Airport in Queens, NY. In his last role with the department, Paul was responsible for the implementation of aviation security policy, managed security technology equipment deployments, and supervised training programs and personnel to enhance the agency's formidable defense against improvised explosive device (IED) threats targeting U.S. aviation assets and infrastructure. Paul earned his M.S. in Homeland Security Management from the Homeland Security and Terrorism Institute at LIU Post, and holds a B.A. in Homeland Security & Emergency Management from Ashford University. He also holds Certificates from the Naval Post Graduate School - Center for Homeland Defense and Security, the Federal Emergency Management Agency (FEMA) and ASIS International. Paul is currently attending the University of Maryland University College and pursuing a M.S. in Cybersecurity. As an active member in the academic, security and emergency management communities, Paul serves as the Advisory Board Chair and Executive Director of the Homeland Security and Security Management program at the Long Island Business Institute in New York. He also serves as an Adjunct Professor under the U.S. Department of Homeland Security – Transportation Security Administration Partnership Program at Erie Community College. Paul previously served as a Visiting Professor at Everest College Phoenix Online where he instructed courses in the University's Criminal Justice program. Paul is a member of the American Society of Industrial Security (ASIS) organization - ASIS International, a member of the International Association of Emergency Managers.

Sara Syed is a Cybersecurity graduate student at University of Maryland Global Campus. Prior to her interests in the Cybersecurity community, she completed her Bachelors degree in Criminal Justice from George Mason University. She has worked for various non-profit institutions in the Washington D.C. area and hopes to inspire more women to join the growing Cybersecurity industry.

Index

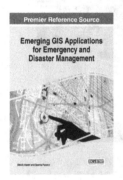

IGI Global Author Services

Providing a high-quality, affordable, and expeditious service, IGI Global's Author Services enable authors to streamline their publishing process, increase chance of acceptance, and adhere to IGI Global's publication standards.

Benefits of Author Services:

- **Professional Service:** All our editors, designers, and translators are experts in their field with years of experience and professional certifications.
- **Quality Guarantee & Certificate:** Each order is returned with a quality guarantee and certificate of professional completion.
- **Timeliness:** All editorial orders have a guaranteed return timeframe of 3-5 business days and translation orders are guaranteed in 7-10 business days.
- **Affordable Pricing:** IGI Global Author Services are competitively priced compared to other industry service providers.
- **APC Reimbursement:** IGI Global authors publishing Open Access (OA) will be able to deduct the cost of editing and other IGI Global author services from their OA APC publishing fee.

Author Services Offered:

English Language Copy Editing
Professional, native English language copy editors improve your manuscript's grammar, spelling, punctuation, terminology, semantics, consistency, flow, formatting, and more.

Scientific & Scholarly Editing
A Ph.D. level review for qualities such as originality and significance, interest to researchers, level of methodology and analysis, coverage of literature, organization, quality of writing, and strengths and weaknesses.

Figure, Table, Chart & Equation Conversions
Work with IGI Global's graphic designers before submission to enhance and design all figures and charts to IGI Global's specific standards for clarity.

Translation
Providing 70 language options, including Simplified and Traditional Chinese, Spanish, Arabic, German, French, and more.

Hear What the Experts Are Saying About IGI Global's Author Services

"Publishing with IGI Global has been *an amazing experience* for me for sharing my research. The *strong academic production* support ensures quality and timely completion." **– Prof. Margaret Niess, Oregon State University, USA**

"The service was *very fast, very thorough, and very helpful* in ensuring our chapter meets the criteria and requirements of the book's editors. I was *quite impressed and happy* with your service." **– Prof. Tom Brinthaupt, Middle Tennessee State University, USA**

www.igi-global.com

Publisher of Peer-Reviewed, Timely, and
Innovative Academic Research Since 1988

IGI Global's Transformative Open Access (OA) Model:
How to Turn Your University Library's Database Acquisitions Into a Source of OA Funding

Well in advance of Plan S, IGI Global unveiled their OA Fee Waiver (Read & Publish) Initiative. Under this initiative, librarians who invest in IGI Global's InfoSci-Books and/or InfoSci-Journals databases will be able to subsidize their patrons' OA article processing charges (APCs) when their work is submitted and accepted (after the peer review process) into an IGI Global journal.

How Does it Work?

Step 1: **Library Invests in the InfoSci-Databases:** A library perpetually purchases or subscribes to the InfoSci-Books, InfoSci-Journals, or discipline/subject databases.

Step 2: **IGI Global Matches the Library Investment with OA Subsidies Fund:** IGI Global provides a fund to go towards subsidizing the OA APCs for the library's patrons.

Step 3: **Patron of the Library is Accepted into IGI Global Journal (After Peer Review):** When a patron's paper is accepted into an IGI Global journal, they option to have their paper published under a traditional publishing model or as OA.

Step 4: **IGI Global Will Deduct APC Cost from OA Subsidies Fund:** If the author decides to publish under OA, the OA APC fee will be deducted from the OA subsidies fund.

Step 5: **Author's Work Becomes Freely Available:** The patron's work will be freely available under CC BY copyright license, enabling them to share it freely with the academic community.

Note: This fund will be offered on an annual basis and will renew as the subscription is renewed for each year thereafter. IGI Global will manage the fund and award the APC waivers unless the librarian has a preference as to how the funds should be managed.

Hear From the Experts on This Initiative:

"I'm very happy to have been able to make one of my recent research contributions *freely available* along with having access to the *valuable resources* found within IGI Global's InfoSci-Journals database."

— **Prof. Stuart Palmer,**
Deakin University, Australia

"Receiving the support from IGI Global's OA Fee Waiver Initiative *encourages me to continue my research work without any hesitation*."

— **Prof. Wenlong Liu**, College of Economics and Management at Nanjing University of Aeronautics & Astronautics, China

For More Information, Scan the QR Code or Contact:
IGI Global's Digital Resources Team at eresources@igi-global.com.

Printed in the United States
by Baker & Taylor Publisher Services